The
Elements of
Epping
Forest

by

Penny Griffiths Morgan

The Elements of Epping Forest

The Elements of Epping Forest

By Penny Griffiths-Morgan

Printed in the United Kingdom

First Printing, 2023

ISBN 9798850586294

Imprint – Independent Published

Published by www.amazon.com

The Elements of Epping Forest

Penny has also written

My Haunted History

A Haunted Experiment

Paranormal Playtimes – The School That Never Sleeps

The Battle for Bosworth Hall

She also is a features writer for Haunted Magazine, has her own podcast called "Haunted Histories" and is a regular Paranormal Historian on shows such as "Help! My House is Haunted"

Contents

The Elements of Epping Forest

Foreword by Jayne Harris

When Penny approached me to write the foreword for her latest book, I was truly honoured and filled with anticipation to delve into her newest creation. This project encapsulates a myriad of subjects that captivate my attention: history, mystery, nature, and, of course, the fabulous Penny herself. It's a combination that is simply irresistible!

I still vividly recall meeting with Penny on the outskirts of Epping Forest last year. It was during the filming of the first season of 'Celebrity Help! My House is Haunted.' As expected, Penny greeted me with her trademark warm smile, accompanied by an exuberant hug. There's something about being in Penny's presence that instantly brightens one's spirits. Surely, I can't be the only one who feels this way, right?

After introducing the crew, we settled down with our coffees, basking in the breathtaking panoramic views. We chatted away until the cameras were ready to roll. At that point, Penny turned to our Series Producer, Ben Cole, with her characteristic directness, asking, "Right, where do you want me to start, and how much do you want?" Her straightforwardness never fails to amuse me.

True to form, she arrived armed with copious notes, photographs, and maps—no one can accuse this sassy historian of lacking thorough research! Indeed, Penny had immersed herself in the history of the area, unearthing every sinister fact imaginable. Surprisingly, despite the obvious natural beauty and serenity of the landscape, there was an abundance of eerie tales waiting to be uncovered.

I must confess that I'm not one to label people's beliefs or persuasions, but for the sake of clarity, I'll adopt a descriptor for myself. As something of a Green Witch, I've always sensed an undeniable, emotive energy resonating through ancient forests. It is within the embrace of trees that I find my greatest sense of peace and grounding. I believe that something primordial still lingers within each of us, and it is this elemental connection that is awakened by experiences such as sitting by an open fire, stargazing, or standing in awe of magnificent Redwood giants.

Having personally researched another spooky woodland, Hagley Woods near Stourbridge, I am no stranger to the potential for macabre tales within such places. As this book will reveal, the hidden music of our ancient forests holds far more than the melodic chorus of birdsong and the gentle rustling of leaves. In her diligent research on Epping Forest, Penny, in her typical fashion, has uncovered lesser-known history, which, to my sinister delight, includes connections to infamous highwaymen and a surplus of grisly deaths.

I have often pondered whether Penny has access to some elusive corner of the dark web where only the most chilling and spine-tingling historical records reside. How else could she take any location, absolutely anywhere, and unveil its unsettling essence as she does? It is a testament to her expertise and knack for uncovering high strangeness.

This book is not merely a collection of intriguing historical facts; it is a guidebook for the intrepid explorer, catering to those who dare to venture deeper into the shadowed side of reality. But tread cautiously, dear wanderer, for as you are about to discover, Epping Forest, despite its alluring beauty, is not for the faint of heart.

And what do Dick Turpin, Queen Victoria, and a German POW have in common? Well, my curious friend, they have all found their place within the pages of this book. So, read on...

By Jayne Harris

Introduction

When you walk into a large established forest, what do you feel? For me, it is a myriad of emotions and experiences which branch deep down into my very soul (pun very much intended). It is the sheer wonderment at how amazing mother nature is. Not to mention the fact that many of the trees have seen hundreds, even thousands of years worth of world events to which they are forever sworn to secrecy.

What if they could talk though, what would they perhaps say? Would they divulge the illicit meetings of two star crossed lovers or would they repeat conversations that had taken place during innocent family rambles?

My guess is that with a little friendly persuasion, their favourite communication would be to tell you just *"who dunnit"* as in decades old murder mysteries.

I guess we will never know, but I have observed that the resounding sense I get when I enter somewhere like Epping Forest is that of being watched…hopefully with some of the things I am going to tell you about in the next few thousand words, you may understand why.

My home has been Essex for - at the time of writing - over twenty-five years and the longer I live here, the more I find out about the county that fascinates me. There is so much more to this ancient Shire than the stereotypical white stiletto and blonde hair jokes, although it was due in part to an Essex based reality show that the idea for this book came about.

I was approached by the producers of Help! My House Is Haunted to provide some historical input on an area in Chigwell, thanks in no small part to the mentioning of my talents by the wonderful Jayne Harris (has the cheque arrived yet?) It was two of the stars of the show "The Only Way Is Essex" that were having their home investigated by the team - how ironic that a programme which has caused me to raise my eyebrow on more than one occasion was also going to give me a chance to disappear into the archives and binge on historical chocolate.

It was after delving into the not unsubstantial past of what is now seen by many as London overspill, and discussing all of my findings with Jayne that she said:

"Blimey, you should write your next book on this…"

So, not being one to look a gift horse in the mouth, I had already started my research into the area and as any writer will tell you, it is that part of the process which inevitably takes a lot more time and resources than the actual scribbling down of thoughts onto paper, I started coming up with a book strategy.

Regular readers of my work – you know who you are, and you are awesome – will appreciate that I try to implement something slightly different in my approach for each book, and I spent a good deal of time staring at the proverbial drawing board in respect of this one. It was while dozing off on the sofa over Christmas 2021 that it came to me, and

The Elements of Epping Forest was created. As you will see as you progress through the book, everything that has happened to this area has links to one of the four elements, whether it be air, fire, earth or water, and it is those connections which make it such a spiritual and ethereal place.

The more research I have done for this new book, the more diversity of events and history has been thrown at me. I know that I am running the risk of sounding patronising but my goal for many of you reading is either to discover something you want to look into more, or even to think broadening my scope when it comes to investigating this beautiful six-thousand acres. There are events to suit every single sensibility, whether it be crime, royalty, the wars and even motorcycle tracks (yes really), I recommend exploring both the area and the options and most importantly, think outside of that cliched box.

I do hope you enjoy what you learn and if you ever visit the forest, say hello to the entities that still call it home.

Chapter 1

The History of the Forest – the early years

Some of the first documented evidence regarding what we now know as Epping Forest was when it was part of a much larger woodland called the Forest of Essex and covered around sixty-thousand acres. Nobody seems to know exactly how old the area is, but they do know that it potentially dates back to at least 60AD and the stories of the infamous Queen Boudica, but more of that later.

To give you an idea as to timelines, I have put the years that each individual monarch ruled in brackets, so if anyone spots them and decides to tell me that their year of birth and year of death are wrong, I know, they are the years they were King (or Queen).

Most tend to start the tales of history from around the 11th century with the arrival of the Normans and the implementation of Forest Law, whereby the then-king, William the Conqueror (ruled 1066 to 1087) had these areas enclosed and made hunting grounds for other Royals and magnates. The impact of this was that a great deal of the ground being used by people as common land, would be now liable to penalties.

When William died, a poem was published in the Peterborough Chronicle 1086 entitled "*The rime of*

King William" which definitely showed this disquiet:

He established many deer preserves
and he set up many laws concerning them
such that whoever killed a hart or a hind
should be blinded.

The control went so far as banning dogs in general from the lands, and if an inhabitant had a guard dog (normally Mastiffs), then their front claws had to be removed, which when you consider the lack of any type of medical knowledge in the 11th century, seems all the more barbaric. What was the penalty of hunting on this land or breaking any of the other rules? According to www.lawi.org.uk, they would lose their hands or be blinded. After the death of William I, it got even worse under the rule of his son, Henry I (1100-1135) and penalties were raised to include death. You may think it would be easy to avoid upsetting the monarchy, after all, Epping Forest is not that big, but consider this, what you see now of the area that the King was deemed to own is now less than a tenth of what it was. Originally, it was one giant area which incorporated the areas that we now know as Waltham Forest, Epping and Hainault. The Naturalist, Oliver Rackham, did some extensive research using the Domesday Book of 1086 and came to the conclusion that the county of Essex consisted of 20% of woodland, which was higher than the country average – according to historians, that figure was nearer 15%. We can safely assume that these Forest Laws would not have been popular, when you think about the number of normal inhabitants on the land (Forests - the legal term for royal hunting grounds - were not just what we would see as a wood under medieval translation and were actually a legal term, they could include land devoid of trees such as pasture) who would not be able to defend their essential crops from the protected animals of the Forest Law from destroying them as the penalties included fencing off areas that the King was allowed to access freely. There were certain wild animals which came under the jurisdiction of the rules as well: Red Deer, Boar, Hare and Wolves...not sure about you, but I do not think I would want to come face to face with a wild boar whilst out walking in Epping Forest!

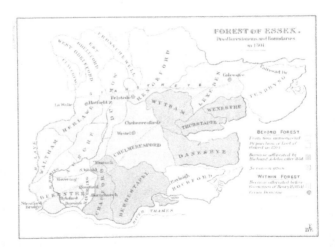

FISHER(1888) p48 - Forest of Essex. Disafforestations and Boundaries in 1301

This map gives you a good idea of just how much of Essex was "forested". You may be familiar with some of the places. I do particularly love the spelling of Chelmeresford and Herlawe…do you recognise them? Chelmsford and Harlow, so those who think of the latter as a new town and only built to take in people bombed out of their homes post World War Two, nope, it has been around a lot longer.

When looking at this, forest does not mean solely woods as I said earlier, and afforesting is to place an area under Forest Law, not to plant more trees which is probably what we would think of now, the term forest having taken on different meaning in the modern world.

It seems that reading through the history books, previous Kings (not Queens, and that is fact not me merely overlooking any feminine control issues) appear to have thrown every single deterrent that they could to try and control people's (mis)use of these forested areas. For example, during the reign of Henry I those penalties I mentioned earlier did not always include death, and poaching from the royal forests was seen to be equal to homicide in the chastisements levied out. There are reports from the time of men being mutilated, having hands and feet chopped off, eyes gauged out and left to die a slow death from hunger as they were unable to feed themselves. This barbaric treatment of people hunting for their food was not just an example of pure cruelty and the joy mankind can take in inflicting assault on each other, but was meant to leave these victims as living walking examples of repercussion.

It is slightly unfair to place all the blame on King Henry I however; many punishments were genuinely condoned and encouraged by other nobility and the Church who enjoyed the benefits of the forests. After all, these poachers affected their pockets and that could not be allowed to go unnoticed.

That is not to say that scholars did not question the logic of the trapping of "beasts" as being punishable. John of Salisbury (scholar, writer, philosopher, Bishop) actually thought it strange because birds flew in the air, and fish swam in the sea so surely they were free and therefore common? But the crown had possession of sturgeon, the head and tail of a whale was expected to be given to the royal consort (not sure how many whales there were in Essex, but we will leave that one unanswered) and bees...all honey would belong to the King if the bees chose to create their hives in the forest!

You may wonder when the bodily harm on poachers was halted? And although we are jumping through the forest timeline somewhat here, it was during the reign of Richard I (1189-1199), the very religious King felt that the desecration of man who was believed to be created in the image of God on account of wild beasts (which according to their belief, were given alike to all and certainly not equal to man) was amoral and sacrilegious, therefore it was abolished and a system of fines, imprisonment and even being forced to leave the country were implemented instead.

In 1215, the unpopular King John (1199-1216) - one which I am not going to give an opinion on whether he was as useless as some historians claim, we have a lot to cover here – was forced to implement the Magna Carta in 1215, and in it were passages relating to forests.

Clause 44 - People who live outside the forest need not in future appear before the **Royal Justices of the Forest** in answer to general summonses, unless they are actually involved in proceedings or are sureties for someone who has been seized for a forest offence.

Clause 47 - All forests that have been created in our reign shall at once be disafforested. River-banks that have been enclosed in our reign shall be treated similarly.

Clause 48 - All evil customs relating to forests and warrens, foresters, warreners, sheriffs and their servants, or river-banks and their wardens, are at once to be investigated in every county by twelve sworn knights of the county, and within forty days of their enquiry the evil customs are to be abolished completely and irrevocably. But we, or our chief justice if we are not in England, are first to be informed.

Clause 52 - To any man whom we have deprived or dispossessed of lands, castles, liberties, or rights, without the lawful judgement of his equals, we will at once restore these. In cases of dispute the matter shall be resolved by the judgement of the twenty-five barons referred to below in the clause for securing the peace (clause 61). In cases, however, where a man was deprived or dispossessed of something without the lawful judgement of his equals by our father King Henry or our brother King Richard, and it remains in our hands or is held by others under our warranty, we shall have respite for the period commonly allowed to Crusaders, unless a lawsuit had been begun, or an enquiry had been made at our order, before we took the Cross as a Crusader. On our return from the Crusade, or if we abandon it, we will at once render justice in full.

Clause 53 - We shall have similar respite [to that in clause 52] in rendering justice in connection with forests that are to be disafforested, or to remain forests, when these were first afforested by our father Henry or our brother Richard; with the guardianship of lands in another person's `fee', when we have hitherto had this by virtue of a `fee' held of us for knight's service by a third party; and with abbeys founded in another person's `fee', in which the lord of the `fee' claims to own a right. On our return from the Crusade, or if we abandon it, we will at once do full justice to complaints about these matters.

John did not survive much longer after the Magna Carta (also known as the Charter of Runnymede) was sealed and his young nine year old son Henry III (1216-1272) inherited the throne (albeit with the guidance until he reached the age of majority of William Marshal, 1st Earl of Pembroke). The young King was only ten years old when the Charter of the Forest 1217 was brought in to supplement his father's Magna Carta. I will not list the whole document as it is very easy to find online if you so choose, but the main gist of it is that if somewhere was afforested and it caused harm to those whose demesne it was, it was to be disafforested. To give you an example, clause 3 stated:

"All woods made forest by king Richard our uncle, or by king John our father, up to the time of our first coronation shall be immediately disafforested unless it be our demesne wood."

Demesne being the land belonging to the Lord of the Manor which was used for his own purposes and not necessarily rented out to tenant farmers etc. There were still some horrific practices to dogs to stop them being able to hunt the "Kings" game, such as clause 6:

"The inquest or view of the expediting of dogs in the forest shall henceforth be made when the regard ought to be made, namely every third year, and then made by the view and testimony of law-worthy men and not otherwise. And he whose dog is then found not expedited shall give as amercement three shillings, and in future no ox shall be seized for failure to expedite. The manner, moreover, of expediting by the assize shall generally be that three claws of the forefoot are to be cut off, but not the ball. Nor shall dogs henceforth be expedited except in places where it was customary to expedite them at the time of the first coronation of king Henry our grandfather"

It was firmed up even further in 1225 when the Forest Charter was re-written, in a nutshell? If land had become forest under Henry II that was not his land to take, it would be given back. Another important clarification was that of grazing animals, if they ventured onto the royal forests they would become the property of the King, but this changed when the charter was read out.

Whilst these rules applied to all the Royal Forests around the country, they would have had huge significance in Essex as such a large amount of the county was afforested and people were unable to function as they would have done. It should be noted however, that Henry did revoke the charter in 1227 under the claim that some of the forests that had been deforested were actually royal lands and therefore should have been left well alone. That theory itself did not work and the charter was brought back in again, and by the early 1300s, the landscape had changed and the area that we would identify as Epping forest was now known as the Forest of Waltham. When Edward IV (1461-1470, 1471-1483) came to power, he noticed that forest law had not been maintained and pulled rank on those who chose to "murder and kyll a nombre of said deare", re-invoking the punishments that had been in place prior of fines, prison sentences and exile.

One of the biggest uses of woodland such as the Forest of Waltham (Epping Forest, or the Forest of Essex) was the money it could produce, and also the vast swathes of timber Mother Nature gave up. Whilst the English navy under Henry VII (1485-1509) was not incredibly grand, his son, Henry VIII (1509-1547) decided to throw all the resources he could into it, and procured most of the building materials from the woods in the south, ready for them to be transported to the ship builders at Woolwich and Deptford. That was not his only use for the forest - hunting was a favoured opulent pastime of many Kings and Henry VIII was no different.

I will be looking at the connection to many Kings and Queens of England and Britain in a subsequent chapter, so I will not focus on them especially here, suffice to say, that in 1630 under

Charles I (1625-1649), they tried to extend the royal forests once more to raise money. If by extending the boundaries of the forest and have them reach just that little bit further was not viable , they ensured that all duties which should have been paid, were. This was not a popular move as you can probably imagine, but it was necessary as there were huge strains on the country's funds.

The next big change was probably during the Civil wars, under the leadership of Lord Protector Oliver Cromwell. Much of the areas in England which were deemed Royal Forests were ordered to be sold, firstly to raise money for the commonwealth. Anything which had belonged to Charles I, his widow, his son or was even in trust and providing them with benefit (be that financial or physical) was to be disposed of for cold hard cash. If you had an interest in purchasing these lands, you were expected to put a bid in to the government. This would have been quite unsettling for many I would have thought, especially as Essex as a county had originally been Parliamentarian, and had then become Royalists again, there must have been genuine concern that they were going to lose homes and such. Fortunately, Cromwell stepped in as Lord Protector and basically vetoed the idea, instead instructing Commissioners to survey all of the royal forests to ascertain how best to use them without too much disruption.

If you read anything about the running of the forests at any stage in its existence, you will hear certain words mentioned which an explanation of which you may find useful - you may even get lucky on an investigation and have one or more come up on a device!

Foresters – these were the Master Keepers, there could be two types, those who were walking Foresters and those who were Yeoman Foresters who would have been on horseback more likely.

Swainmote – a court held before the verderers of the forest, this would be held three times a year.

Verderer – the officials who made sure the forests were governed accordingly, they would deal with more minor offences with the Justice taking on the more serious ones. Epping forest still has verderers now who help to maintain and preserve the forest.

Lord Warden – Chief officer governing the specific forest.

Justice of the Forest - The person (male) who oversaw all of forest law.

Hundred – administrative division.

Purpresture – other uses of land, such as building structures, this was said in an accusatory way as opposed to purely descriptive.

Assarting – the clearing of land for farming.

Bailiwick – district or jurisdiction.

Regarder - a body of twelve knights whose role it was to inspect the forests every three years or so to ensure no one was encroaching on the Kings lands.

Ranger of the Purlieu – the Purlieu was the area at the edge of the forest, which although officially governed by the forest law, land was allowed to be farmed and deer killed under certain circumstances. It was the Ranger's role to ensure that this happened in accordance with the rules.

With regard to the latter, I can give you some of the names to whom this role was attributed –

1709 John Wroth

1718 Lord Castlemain

1722 John Goodere

1763 Anthony Bacon

1786 Sir William Smijth

1811 Charles Smith

1814 William Matthew Raikes

1830 William St Julien Arabin

1831 Sir Emmanuel Felix

Following the Civil War, and the restoration, the habit of using the forest for hunting and similar pursuits by the monarchy started to wain and there were more issues with regards to inclosures (enclosures) and land being removed from commoner use.

Even though this period was very encouraging of disforestation, from 1713 there were Courts of Attachment every forty days (also known as forty day court or Woodmote) that were held to look at crimes committed against forest law and were presided over by the Verderers and warden (or their deputy). These courts were held at the Kings Head in Chigwell (the very same Old

Maypole from Barnaby Rudge and the place visited by TOWIE as Sheesh…) and the rolls have the same introduction every time, which from 1713 to 1733 and a few years into the rule of George II (1727 to 1760) was in Latin. Licenses were given out for things like hunting, felling trees, ordering horses and goats from the forest, but in one, a man by the name of John Little was brought forward for enclosing ground in Chadwell Heath - twenty-six yards in length and eighteen yards breadth. This shows how far the forest actually spread if you know the geography of Essex.

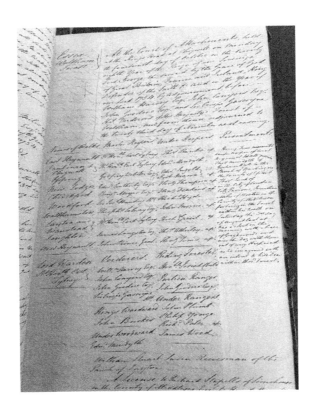

Copy of a court of attachment hearing, photo author's own.

In fact, the area spread even further than people may envisage looking at greater London now, during the "perambulations" of Charles I (1625-1649) the forest is said to have started from the bridge at Stratford known as Bow Bridge over the River Lea, just over two miles from the historical Royal Exchange – it is hard to comprehend, is it not?

I touch on the evacuation of the East End into nearby Epping in another chapter, but Epping Forest was also cited as a place for emergency camps to be established at the outbreak of the Second World War, should the need to get people out of the riskier areas arise. The authorities did guess that people might try and escape the horror of the dock areas (and we do know how hard they were hit) for the sanctity and peace of the woods. A camp commandant (Mr. B.S. Mannock of Ivy Lodge, Epping) was hired, and then volunteers were called for, one hundred in total. Interestingly, they were mainly created for those in the education profession from schools like Buckhurst Hill County Grammar, the technical colleges in Barking and Walthamstow, Loughton High School for Girls and Ilford County School. Two different sites were established, one at Fairmead Bottom and the other near to Copped Hall, with an estimated capacity of fifty thousand. The whole idea was to stop the probability of people flocking into the area without any order and enable the recording of who was where. In fact, one of the letters between the various officials specifically stated that they needed to keep "aliens, deserters, Irishmen and others who they desire contact with..." out of the camps to stop them getting lost in the system.

Apologies to anyone Irish (or Alien?) This was genuinely what the September 1939 document said:

The infrastructure was designed to look after people for one night at a time, the camps would be cleared every day, the stay was not to be long term, but canteens were established at Wake Arms Riding School and Fairmead Bottom. (*Metropolitan police records, war measures WW2)

Read on through the other chapters following this for even more of the history of the forest, how it changed through the Kings and Queens of this country, and the things it has seen.

Chapter Two

Myths and Legends of the Forest

It is perhaps unsurprising that somewhere so full of energy and wonder as a huge wooded area would have such myriad folklore and fact attributed to it. I admit happily to being one of those weird people who walks into an area full of trees and natural history, with a huge smile plastered across my face, who then proceeds to touch and hug these wonderful examples of Mother Nature's work.

Sorry, is that too "hippy" for you? Are you looking for more fact and history? I did digress (which I will confirm I did a lot of whilst researching for this book, a lot of beautiful trees were spoken to and smiled at. Who says writing is a chore?)

Anyway, back to myths and legends of the area we now know as Epping Forest. I am not covering these in chronological order, they are going to be discussed in whichever kind of organised chaos that both my notes and my mind throw up to me. Hopefully I will teach you about a few you did not know, and maybe if there are some I have not mentioned, you would be able to return the favour to me?

The first is that of highway robbery, one that for some conjures up romantic images of misunderstood men galloping away on horseback after stealing whatever they could from the dastardly male of the house and leaving the poor women swooning in their wake. Once you start learning about it however, any whimsical ideas you may have about it such as devilishly handsome creatures like Adam Ant telling people to "stand and deliver" whilst they intend no harm whatsoever, soon start to fade away and you realise many of these people were true hardened criminals.

This type of crime has been in existence since roads were first constructed, but it was during the first half of the 17th century that it really became popular. The traditional grandiose costume of a highwayman (although not all wore it) - and please excuse me assuming all robbers were male, there were a few females, but not as many – was not dissimilar to the uniform worn by the Royalist soldiers and supporters of the English Civil war, and this parallel is not just something that I am plucking out of thin air - many of the earlier protagonists were in actual fact passionate Royalists who stated that they only robbed followers of Cromwell, and would allow anyone who was against the Parliamentarians to go free.

The area of Epping forest would have been a godsend to those wishing to carry out this sort of crime, keeping in mind that it was much bigger than what you see now, and also contained the original London to Newmarket road - so the thoroughfare bringing back those gambling winnings from the racecourse was always ripe for rich pickings. We can go back further than the infamous Dick Turpin (more of him shortly, obviously, as probably the region's most famous villain) for evidence of these crimes for in 1617, the locals were so fed up of the constant threat of being attacked when traversing the road I mentioned that they went toe to toe with the resident robbers. In the end, five highwaymen were injured and one killed. This did not deter the legend of the highway thief however, and in 1698, a group of demobbed soldiers decided to form the "Highwaymen's colony" in part of the forest near Waltham Cross.

Poets and writers of the time are always useful when assessing the history of an era, and in a book by William Addison called *Epping Forest: Its literary and Historical Associations,* he mentions a poet called John Byrom (1692 -1793) who wrote a ballad about being held up in the forest. It is quite long, but here is one of the verses which paints a good picture as to why people were so terrified when on a coach trip and why so many wrote a Last Will and Testament before even the shortest of journeys.

Now then, as fortune had contriv'd, our way
Thro' the wild brakes of Epping Forest lay:
With travellers and trunks a hugeous load
We hagg'd along the solitary road
Where nought but thickets within thickets grew
No house nor barn to cheer the wand'ring view
Nor lab'ring hind nor shepherd did appear
Nor sportsman with his dog or gun was there
A dreary landscape bushy and forlorn
Where rogues start up like mushrooms in a morn

There was even an opera written called "The Beggars Opera" by John Gay in 1728 which revolves around a highwayman named MacHeath - a character that Gay had based on the very well-known Jack Shepperd, who was a thief, bigamist, philanderer and prison escapee. This was definitely an area that was used for entertainment, which is possibly also why people almost glamourised the antiheroes, made these cold and calculating villains handsome and desirable.

Epping and the surrounding area does seem to be quite proud of its highwaymen history, unfortunately this pub in Theydon Bois on the outskirts of the forest no longer exists, but it was named after a colourful character called Jack Rann. He was a highwayman who would wear sixteen coloured strings or silks on his breeches and although he was not caught for committing crimes in the Epping area, he was executed at Tyburn in 1774 at the age of just twenty-four years old. The Derby Mercury published a piece about Jack on 9th December 1774, laying the blame for his change of career from postillion to highwayman firmly at the door of his female love. Apparently, she had been used to being spoiled and having money spent on her as a mistress by her previous "nobleman" paramour, and he needed to find cash and fast to keep her interested.

Is the use of Epping Forest as a hidey hole for those uttering "stand and deliver" fact or fiction, however? Very much fact - I went through some of the records from the Chelmsford Assizes and found quite a few names who were executed for that particular reason between the 1760s and up to around 1820 at least. In August 1819, nineteen-year-old Edward Wright was hanged after his crimes in the forest, but he was not the only person to have a date with the gallows that day. He was accompanied by brothers Joseph and John Merrington (burglary) and J. Tubbs (burglary), and not one of these men were over twenty-two years of age.

William Dench was executed on the 11th August 1797 after he had robbed one John Laundy seven months prior, of around £27 (about £4,000 in today's money or thereabouts). What is unusual about Dench is that he actually ran the George Inn pub in Chelmsford, and after his body was cut down from the gallows he was carried upon a brewers dray, with his favourite grey horse leading, flanked by four brewers in their smocks until he was interred in nearby Widford.

I know you have all been waiting for the most famous highwayman son of Essex, Richard Turpin. Born in 1705 in Hempstead (near Saffron Walden), he started off his working life as a butcher, but was soon suspected of stealing cattle and cutting them up for onward sale. After a short while he decided that crime was going to pay far better than earning a genuine living; he had been supplied with poached deer by the Gregory Gang, so went to work with them. They soon migrated from butchery of animals to that of people. One particularly vicious assault was perpetrated upon an elderly widow. Turpin is said to have shouted at the old woman when she refused to give up the location of her valuables "God damn your blood you old bitch, if you won't tell us, I'll set your bare arse on the grate." The witness (a member of the gang who turned witness to escape a death penalty) confirmed they did just that until the poor lady gave in.

There were more tales of assault with the gang, and even rape (although not by Turpin it has to be said, he was more into actual or grievous bodily harm than sexual assault). After the group were caught, Turpin managed to escape into the forest, and although he did try to stay legal for a while, the pull of crime was too strong. However, the person he tried to rob was actually an infamous highwayman himself, one Matthew King (also known as Tom). Perhaps with good sense, Turpin decided to join forces with King, and they had quite a successful partnership robbing carriages around London and even into the outskirts of Suffolk.

One of the old forest roads, Epping forest, photo author's own

But what of some of the more fanciful stories - could they be real? At one point Turpin, early in his career but already gaining some genuine notoriety, would hide in a cave in High Beach. He was hidden away by the detritus of the forest and would venture down to meet his wife who would provide him with food. 19th century excavationists claimed to have found this cave and turned it into a small pub called Turpin's Cave, and they used to brag that the items they had displayed on their walls (padlocks, flintlock pistol, rusty handcuffs and such-like) were found in the cave when they took over. It is now a housing estate, so probably all traces of Turpin's time there have been paved over.

Another story about Turpin, also known as John Palmer, revolves around the infamous Black Bess – no, he did not ride from Epping to York in three hours - you would struggle to drive it in that time, let alone gallop the same horse for over two hundred and fifty miles! He was an accomplished horseman, and his ride was that which would get him away from anyone trying to capture him. He had a stable behind an old house in Buckhurst Hill called Luctons (no longer there), but he also had another on the first floor of the home which was found by going through the bedroom. Legend has it then when Dick had gone on a mad gallop back to the house, he would have a second identical horse in the accessible stall and his sweating steed would be hidden away in the house, thereby assuring the Kings men that there was no way it could have been Gentleman Dick who they had just chased…

mariborougn promijes 100 Guineas. W. L.

On Wednefday Night laft, a Servant of Mr. Thompfon's, one of the Keepers of Epping Foreft, (who lives at Fair-Maid Bottom) faw the famous Turpin on the Foreft, and fufpecting he was going to fteal fome particular Horfe in that Neighbourhood, went to a Houfe near King's Oak and borrow'd a Gun, and charg'd it, and faid he would go and take Turpin, who was not far off, and accordingly went with the Gun after him; but approaching him with his Gun too near (apprehending, tis fuppos'd, he had only Piftols) Turpin faw him, and immediately difcharg'd a Carbine at him, loaded with Slugs, and fhot him into the Belly dead on the Spot, and he now lies at the Oak: Turpin rode away and quitted his Horfe, which was laft Night in the Pound at Waltham Abby. On Thurfday all that part of the Country were up in Arms in purfuit of him, but its fuppofed he is gone North-

Newcastle Courant 14th May 1737

As this book is about Epping, I can tell you that Turpin did indeed escape north, started calling himself John Palmer and was executed in York on the 7th April 1739.

The next myth is very different and incredibly sad: that of the suicide pool. One of the things I noticed when I was researching to talk about Epping Forest for the episode of *Help! My House is Haunted* was the unusual amounts of drownings there had been. Suicide is such a difficult and sensitive subject to talk about, but I would have expected more deaths to be from hanging or shooting than using water in a wooded area. This led me to the legend of the suicide pool, an area in the forest (which I will not divulge nor visit). The story goes back to the seventeenth century; a young couple would meet by this body of water to conduct their forbidden affair. The young woman's father found them and killed her in disgust at the man she was courting, and her lover, distraught at her death took his own life there and then, and supposedly the water turned black and murky, and all the surrounding vegetation wilted to brown waste and all around the water's edge and dead animals started to appear.

Many articles telling of this legend talk of a young woman by the name of Emma Morgan, who was discovered here with her baby, having taken her own life with no-one knowing why...I decided to look into this particular double death to find out if there was more to it, or could it be that evil spirits in the water lured her to her demise?

Emma had been working as a maid for one Mr. Davis of 4 Northumberland Park, Tottenham for a few years when she discovered she was pregnant. It seems Mr. Davis' first name was William, and he was a licensed victualler, married to Elizabeth and with a son also called William. Miss Morgan went to the workhouse in 1858 at Edmonton to have her child, a son, but quite soon discharged herself and was secured accommodation by a representative of Mr. Davis at York St. North in Hackney. The next witness reports state that she left there after falling out with the landlady and told anyone who would listen that she would go back to the Union in order for the child's father to take responsibility for his actions. Both her and the little baby boy were not discovered for a short while, and it was not until mid -January 1859 that they were identified as twenty-two-year-old Emma Morgan, step daughter of Robert Oswell the lock keeper at Enfield. There were two boys born at Enfield in 1858 who had the same surname as their mother (a good indicator of a single parent), one was called Arthur, and the other? William. The official cause of death was put down as suicide, but I would be questioning a couple of things here: the fact the child was called William (the same name as her previous employer and his son), the fact that the former employer secured her accommodation, also there were those witness reports of her wanting to out the father to make him pay for his child.

Nevertheless, Emma is now associated with the legend of this pool – whether her death truly was suicide or not.

Another water related death which ended up written down as "possible" suicide was that of William Silwood, a newly sworn-in forest keeper who was dealing with poaching cases in 1909. Born in 1864, he joined the army at the age of eighteen and had an incredibly distinguished career with the 2nd Life Guards, including fighting in the Boer war and received a Distinguished Conduct Medal. He joined the Essex Imperial Yeomanry in 1901, and when he retired from there in 1909, he began his career working in Epping. On the night of the 1st November 1909 (or it could have been 31st October, reports are not conclusive) his wife Caroline notified his superiors that he had not returned home, and he was subsequently discovered face down in a small body of water in Monks wood. The cause of death was deemed to be suffocation due to drowning, but no wounds or marks were found on him to suggest how this tall (over six foot) tenured military man had been overcome, if that was the case. The sad tale left a widow and nine children, seven of which were under sixteen years old.

There are other more recent tales of tragedy associated with the woods and people who have felt no other choice but to end their lives, but I am not going to mention those and will finish instead with the sad tale of William Barnes. During the 1930's, Great Britain was undergoing an economic downturn (as were many other parts of the world), and it was hard for people to find work, especially if you were slightly older and had anything wrong with you. Although unemployment by 1934 had started to reduce, and new benefits for those who were unable to find work were introduced by the second half of the year, there were still struggles for those who fell through the net. It transpires that William (and yes, I have noticed this chapter mentions the name William a lot) was sixty years old, a labourer who had struggled to find work for some time and had recently discovered he was losing his sight. His friends said he was very depressed, and it was, although tragic, no surprise when in May 1934 his body was discovered in Connaught Water in the forest.

I hope you do not mind my digressing slightly here, but if you ever feel that suicide is your only option, please do reach out and talk to someone first, the Samaritans in the UK on 116 123, in the United States on 1 (800) 273-TALK or Australia on 135 247.

Continuing with the myths and legends of Epping forest, we're going back a few years now to the invasion of England by the Romans and the amazing stand of resistance by the Iceni, and specifically Queen Boudica.

One of the interesting facts I learned about this phenomenal warrior was that most people know her as Boadicea, and there was no way her name would have been that as (advised to me by my fellow historian Lucy Willgress) as the Celts did not have a soft "c" in their language, so Celts is pronounced "kelt" and not "selt". From then on I have made a real effort to write Boudica (so Booo – di- ka) rather than some of the other variations of her name.

Some fast facts about Boudica: who she was and why she rebelled against the Romans...are you ready? Her husband was Prasutagus, and they were King and Queen of the Iceni tribe of East Anglia (predominantly Norfolk) and in order to protect his Kingdom, Prasutagus had arranged with the Roman rule that on his death, half of his estate would go to the Emperor and the other half would go to his two daughters with Boudica.

Simple right? Well, when he died the Romans did not abide by his will or the agreement and flogged his wife and raped his daughters, so it's not really surprising that his widow was a tad annoyed and decided to wreak havoc.

In AD60/61 (no one is quite sure of the exact year) Boudica commanded a revolt against the Roman rule. She created allies in other Celtic tribes including the Trinovantes who had seen their capital of Colchester (Camulodunum in Roman terms) taken, and that was the first place they attacked. Legend has it they burned it to the ground; this destruction would have been very symbolic for the Romans as it was where a lot of retired Roman soldiers were based. The "rebels" then marched onto Londinium (London) levelling it as they went to their next target of Verulamium (St. Albans to you and I). All in all, contemporary historians estimated at least seventy thousand people (men, women and children) were killed in the battles, and many were brutally tortured with parts of their bodies cut off and then sewn onto other limbs.

The Roman general Suetonius had to stop her, and what happened is something known as the Battle of Watling Street. This was the old road built by his fellow countrymen that took you from London to Wroxeter in Shropshire. Here's the thing however, nobody truly knows where this battle took place, all we know is that it was the scene of Boudica's defeat and some believe her suicide - her daughters dying with her.

The myth relating to our forest, however, is that it was the site of her final camp, the place where the final showdown between her and Suetonius took place, and also where the life drained out of her and the two children. Could this be true?

Fact is, there are two Iron Age camps in the forest, of that there is no dispute, Loughton Camp and Ambresbury Banks. The former is where she is meant to have spent the last night before the final battle…the latter, where she died. Do I think that it is plausible? No, I have attached a map below showing the three places she sacked - why would she have gone backwards from St. Albans to Epping, and then marched towards the Midlands where Watling Street is marked? It is far more logical that the Epping visit was either between Colchester and London, or London and St. Albans. Could she have camped there? Very probably, there would have been safety and food in the woods, and plenty of materials to make new weapons or repair old ones. She would have been hidden from the Roman armies and there is more evidence of there being more Celt tribes than the invaders, as her allies the Trinovantes governed a lot of Essex and the Catuvellauni (whose centre was at Verulamium) were the other.

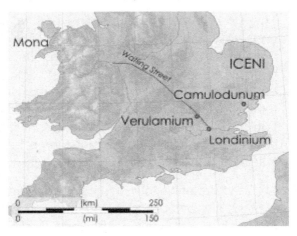

https://archive.org/details/newstudentsatlas00reicuoft/page/n17/mode/2up?view=theater *by Amitchell125*

So looking at the map, if Boudica's last stand was not in Epping forest, the myth that she drowned her daughters and poisoned herself amongst the trees is unlikely to have any credence, but that does not mean her spirit may not still be there…after all, the energy that she must have generated before leading her troops to such amazing victories would have been immense and it may not have dissipated.

Is your desire for the myths and legends of the forest satiated yet? Well, if you want more, I can give a few more...

This next story is one that I have heard recounted many times, but I have not been able to find its original source or who reported it. The sighting has links to the Queen Boudica account I mentioned earlier, but also the history of water-related paranormal activity around the forest in general.

Running through Epping is a thoroughfare called Lindsey Street (now the B181), and the legend is that in the 1960's, some people saw ghostly figures on horseback emerging from the pond and galloping off...some accounts describe them as being dressed in ancient costumes and others more Cavalier type – which is entirely possible, as the Royalists did indeed march through Epping on their way to Colchester for the siege of Colchester in 1648.

I will freely admit to drawing a complete blank when I tried to find more information regarding this, such as which pond and who had seen this apparition, so I turned to social media and a fantastic Facebook group called History of Epping Photographs. The admin, Wendy, kindly posted about it and we got a few replies. She told me that the story she had always been told was that an old-fashioned milk man driving his cart fell asleep and accidentally directed the vehicle into the water. Apparently he reappeared missing his head, and is seen every so often coming out of the water and along Lindsey Street – sometimes towards the Epping Cemetery.

The site is known as Knocker's Pond, and not only was it the main water source for about a quarter of the town in the 19th century (and the reported cause of enteric fever, or typhoid, to many), it was also where a few suicides took place.

Whether that is where the stories have come from, or if some typical form of whispers have mutated the original incident to what I have been told, and all children growing up in the Epping area get given it as a "spooky" bedtime story talking about the scary pond, I know not.

The Essex Newsman in March 1878 carried a small piece about one of these deaths. Early one morning Mr. Bates' milk boy was passing Knockers Pond and saw a neatly folded coat with a hat placed on top, so he stopped and found a letter underneath:

My Dear Brother - When you receive this, my body will be lying in the pond at the lane near Epping. My brain is gone mad through that cursed horse racing and betting. I have spent my last penny in the town for bread, but I am driven mad through Croydon races. Please break the news to my unhappy wife and children. Tell her I have found her last words came true. Keep this from poor father, it will break his heart. Good bye, my brother Walter; if it is possible never remember me no more.—From your unhappy brother, Walter Morris - tell Bill Farridy to give up betting

They dragged the pond but found no body, and although a telegram was sent to the addressee of the letter, a Mr. Thomas Morris, no reply was ever received. Did he really exist? There are quite a few Walter Morris' from Lancashire, but the 1871 census does show a Thomas Morris living at Peter Street in Manchester which was the address shown on the letter. He was not a greengrocer however, but a publican yet sadly the 1881 census shows his wife as a widow, it seems he passed away the year after his "brother".

Was I able to track down any first account sightings though with the assistance of the helpful Facebook page? Well that is the thing, two people came forward who had experiences of seeing things from the pond. One person (who has not given me permission to say their name) recollected that in the early 1980's, they were coming home late at night, and saw something emerge from the pond and disappear into the shadows. They were so unnerved by what they saw, that they did not tell anyone about it for months as they were scared they would be ridiculed.

A slightly more comprehensive account came from Scott Barker. He told me:

As far as I can recall myself, Ian Bowes, Simon Fuller and a few others had been in Harlow for the evening and had arrived back in Epping around 10pm and rather than go our separate ways home we decided to walk up to Epping Green to see if we could find a couple more mates to hang around with despite us all more or less agreeing that it would be an unsuccessful mission. We made our way down Lindsey street and were just laughing and larking about. As we passed the last of the houses it seemed to get a bit misty and felt quite cold but not really more than you'd expect on a late Autumn evening/ night. Nobody said a lot as we passed the area of Knocker's Pond until someone commented on the cold and said it felt a bit odd, and we all agreed that the atmosphere seemed to have changed a bit and that we all felt a bit on edge but we carried on along the road and the fog seemed to have got a bit more thick, we kept going but decided that we would continue along the road but give the Epping Green mission a miss and instead head back to Epping via Bury Lane and the Black Pond. As we passed the Epping Green turn off, we kept thinking a car was coming along because of lights but no cars actually came and passed us and we started to feel frightened and we agreed that it started to feel different from the moment we passed Knocker's Pond. We were all fairly spooked by then and then a car passed us from the Bury Lane end and as it passed in the fog I looked at the car as it passed and its headlights picked out what looked like a horse and buggy, I asked if anyone else had seen it and the question was answered by us all immediately running and looking behind at something that was flickering on and off but definitely had the shape of a cart and driver. We were all scared and fairly out of breath by the time we reached the Black Pond and the thatched cottage and considered cutting across the fields to Tower Road but it was too scary and so we stayed on the road as the fog was less. We didn't linger near the cemetery and made our way to Ian Bowes' house, and recalled all our feelings about the experience. The following night we set off with a larger group of people from the Bury Lane end to see if we could see it again but we saw nothing, but the word spread and a few nights later there were about fifty people meeting by the cemetery to do the walk around but the police turned up and wanted to know what the big crowd was about, and we told them and I guess they told the West Essex Gazette who interviewed myself and the original mates and did a story, and subsequently we learned of the coachman ghost that supposedly haunts the area near Knocker's Pond. Where we saw our ghost was nearly at the bottom of Bury Lane, but for sure it was the same phantom. I still have an open mind about ghosts and believe there's something to hauntings.

I asked Scott how old they were, late teens was the answer. Was this the reason that the apparition was able to manifest, that their teenage exuberance gave it the energy?

It is quite difficult to follow that for sure, but here is another tale that even made the newspapers back in 1908. Either it was a slow news day, or there had been other occurrences of this particular incident that had not yet made it into print. The forest itself covers a huge area as you are probably aware by now, and each little bit has its own name for identification purposes. The part I am going to mention is known as Warren Hill and is a stone's throw from Connaught Waters and also Queen Elizabeth's hunting lodge. There is a path that makes its way through the canopy of trees, linking Manor Road to Warren Hill, and apparently late one evening in June 1908, a gentleman was making his way home from work in Chingford to Loughton by cutting through the woodland. He reported that he felt something strike him on his back, and a heavy object connect with his cheek leaving a minor injury, but when he turned to see who - or what – was attacking him, there was no-one there. Whilst I could not find any other documentation around this, the news article specifically states "a series of assaults on pedestrians" which certainly implies this was not the only one.

Being the intrepid explorer that I am, and also accompanied by my very large dog, I took a walk through this part of Epping Forest to see if anything wanted to try and scare me away...have a look at the chapter on investigations if you want to see what we found.

The last legend of the forest that I am going to mention is that of William Bell, also known as Dr. Bell and less politely, Old Dido. He was quite well known in the area of Hainault Forest, and the area of Chigwell. He tells people he was born in March 1831, and was originally from Bethnal Green in London, orphaned by the age of eleven, he had a variety of jobs, working as a fish seller and also a labourer in the East India Docks – which unsurprisingly, given the lack of health and safety back then, caused him to have more than a few accidents including one which he said he was left for dead. In 1880 (according to the newspaper reports of the time) he decided to move out to the forest and created his own makeshift dwelling with a tarpaulin strung between two trees and a bed of rags, but it was his new vocation for which he became known. Bell never begged, he reinvented himself as a herbalist and would sell his products to locals, and also repaired the hedges and ditches as his "payment" for living in the forest. Whilst it appears that the locals were quite content with his alternative lifestyle (he would also go blackberry picking and then walk to London to sell them) in the 1901 census he was recorded as Dr.

Bell, herbal doctor and his address being a tent in the forest.

Even the Chelmsford Chronicle Newspaper said on the 8th August 1902 that he seemed "better off than tens of thousands of his congeners in the East End slums who breathe the foulest air and live under the most depressing conditions". Someone, however, was not happy with his choice of residency, and in June 1904 Bell returned to his shelter to find it torn down, and the garden he had carefully cultivated for the last twenty-five years or so, absolutely destroyed. The nearby people of Chigwell, who he had seen on a daily basis and helped with his remedies let him sleep in open ground there, many were upset by the fact he had been forcibly evicted from a place where he was doing no harm whatsoever.

It is hard to trace what happened to him after that, he does not appear in the 1911 census so one can assume he had passed away by that point. The only William Bell who is marked as deceased was in the 2nd quarter of 1911, and his place of death was West Ham. Whether it is our self- made herbalist I am not sure, but there were many people who would have been sad to see him leave.

Chapter 3 - From the Air

Now on to a subject I enjoy getting the chance to talk about...things that happen in the sky.

With an area covering nearly six-thousand acres, we have a vast expanse to cover that is classed as Epping Forest these days, and I am taking us to less than one-hundred years ago for this chapter, starting in 1939. I must caveat my comment about enjoying talking about aviation with the fact that not all of these things I am going to talk about are pleasant in any way and do involve tragic deaths.

I do not think you can look at the gigantic area known as Epping Forest without a chapter on airfields and the world wars.

Based nearby is North Weald airfield, if you do not know it as a centre of flying, you may remember there being a huge market that took place on a Saturday every week – although personally every time I visit, it is in the hope that one of the vintage aircraft based there is going up for a recce and I can stand and watch like the aircraft stalker that I am. Its history is quite long, back in 1916, it set up as Royal Flying Corps Station North Weald Bassett to help defend London from the Zeppelins which were being launched from Germany. There were lots of these bases dotted around the U.K. There had to be as the aircraft used had incredibly small fuel tanks and would need regular topping up...on the 1st April 1918, it passed over to the R.A.F. and started to be developed and built up ready as a major contender on the defence (and attack) front. When you visit the area now, take a moment to drive around and see what obvious M.O.D. type buildings you can spot - there are quite a few.

I digress, around the middle of 1938, No. 56 Squadron, that was based there took their first delivery of Hawker Hurricane aircraft, a type of fighter which was going to become synonymous with the Second World War even though it is overshadowed by its little brother, the Supermarine Spitfire - do not get me started on which is superior, or we would be here for hours!

On Monday 12th June, 1939, three Hurricane aircraft had taken off from R.A.F. North Weald, when the lead flier, Pilot Officer Montague Hulton-Harrop reported that they were only a mile or so away from base, and climbing from around three hundred feet when the machine that Pilot Officer Peter Charlton was flying suddenly reared up underneath him, striking his wing. Within seconds P.O. Charlton's aircraft had fallen away, hitting the trees in the Thornwood area of Epping, and burst into flames. Soldiers from the Essex Yeomanry were stationed near to the crash site and ran to try and help the pilot but were unable to get near the wreckage due to the immense heat. Even when the R.A.F. fire tender arrived, they struggled to deal with the inferno in their protective suits. Tragically, P.O. Charlton died in hospital soon after, his crash and burn injuries proving fatal. I think that there was a case of fate knowing what was in store however, because on 6th September 1939, less than three months later, P.O. Hulton-Harrop was involved in a friendly fire incident with members of No. 74 Squadron based at R.A.F. Rochford (a satellite of R.A.F. Hornchurch). Two squadrons had been dispatched from North Weald - 56 and 151 – as the searchlight batteries spotted an enemy formation appearing over the sea. The Spitfires of 74 Squadron mistook the Hurricanes of North Weald as BF 109's and were given the order to attack. The pilot who accidentally shot down Hulton-Harrop never forgot the incident, and even though nineteen- year-old P.O. Freeborn became a Wing Commander, earned a Distinguished Flying Cross and was classed as a fighter ace during the Battle of Britain, he always kept that dreadful day in his mind. It was known as The Battle of Barking Creek.

Later on in the war, North Weald became home to some Norwegian squadrons, in fact, two of those pilots would become very well known for reasons other than flying…this is a copy of an article I wrote for Haunted Histories which you may find interesting.

The Great Escape

I am going to start this piece of writing really badly with a question…how many of you try and find some verification for anything you get given when on an investigation? It probably would not surprise you to know that I do, nearly every single time, and whilst the information is rarely there, when it is, it certainly makes you go "woah" (Bill & Ted style).

On Friday 16th July, I was lucky enough to get the opportunity to do a talk on the Air Transport

Auxiliary (A.T.A.) at the Haunted Antiques Paranormal Research Centre. After I had finished speaking, we were able to conduct some investigations of the museum. For those of you who have not heard of the A.T.A. (a.k.a. Ancient and Tattered Airmen or Anything to Anywhere), they were the amazing brave souls who transported all the aircraft during World War Two. The room I was most drawn to at the centre was the War room, or the military room, whatever you want to call it, and when we began to do some investigations, I was joined at the ouija board there by Karen, Dave, Chris and Louise. The latter was taking photographs throughout - more of that in a bit, whilst the four of us were sat around the table. Quite soon, a "spirit" came through who introduced himself as Peter and said he had been a fighter pilot in World War Two. When it came to him spelling out what he had flown, it did not make sense, for some reason I asked him if he was Norwegian…yes, came the answer. This confused me as at the time, I do not know why Norway popped into my head, for a pilot Polish may have been a more logical call, but Norway?

The others started asking him questions and he seemed very reluctant to answer anything that may have been deemed war-related, at that point Dave said "maybe he was a prisoner of war?" Nothing in the room was related to that as far as we were aware, then we asked him if he was related to any of us, no came the answer. Was he attracted to one of us? It shot to yes.

"Please take the glass to the person who you are drawn to…" at that point, Dave took his finger off the glass and it literally shot towards me, nearly flying off the table. Well okay then, I thought, the military magnet has not lost her touch! As the evening progressed, it transpired that "Peter" would only talk to me, and had been based at North Weald airfield; I must admit that I knew there was a Norwegian contingent there, but that was about the sum of my knowledge regarding that.

We asked him if he knew when he had passed, and the answer "6" and "9" came out, either 1969 or age sixty-nine, we assumed. There was another interesting fact however, when we talked about a wife, the glass spelled out "Peg".

That was that, I thought. A Norwegian fighter pilot called Peter who flew from North Weald and who died with the numbers six and nine having some relevance.

On the Sunday after, I started researching and even writing this, I am shaking with disbelief. The first thing I did was look for Norwegian pilots based at R.A.F. North Weald called Peter. Obviously Peter is the anglicised version of "Per", the only Per I could find was Per Bergsland who had changed his name to Peter Rockland to protect his family when he was taken prisoner by the Germans after bailing out during the raid at Dieppe and taken into Stalag Luft III – yes, the same prison camp that 'The Great Escape' happened from.

Then it gets even more amazing. I mean, if you are going to speak to a former Prisoner of War, speak to one who was one of the three who managed to make it back home! The film (whilst brilliant) does not tell you about the two

Norwegians and the one Dutchman who were the sole successful escapees (he made it back with fellow North Weald pilot Jens Muller, the Dutchman was Bram Van der Stok. Of the seventy-six who made the attempt, seventy-three were recaptured and fifty of those executed.

Per/Peter made it to safety, so what I hear you say? It may not have been him, but here is the clincher in my mind: Per Bergsland died in 1992...on June 9th – 6/9. If you want further validation of this, Bergsland's wife was called Margarete, the name Peg or Peggy is derived from Margaret.

Was I talking to pilot Per Bergsland, one of only three fliers to make it out of those tunnels alive? I do not know.

If you want to learn more about North Weald, and the operations it flew, I would strongly suggest visiting the museum www.nwamuseum.co.uk which is based in the old Commanding Officers house.

Many of the crashes which took place from the air, and landed in the Forest area were German aircraft. To help you with the abbreviations I am going to use, I have listed at the back of this book a guide, which also shows the equivalent position in the R.A.F. (as close as we can get them).

The three Luftwaffe crashes I am going to mention here, all happened in 1940, and all were fatal (aside from one survivor who was taken into a Prisoner of War camp).

On 3rd September, 1940, a terrific dog fight was taking place over the circuit of R.A.F. North

Weald, the Luftwaffe had taken to attacking fighter bases at this point to put them out of action and give their bombers safe passage into the U.K. Whether there was some momentary incapacitation, or pure pilot mistake, two Messerschmitt ME110's collided with each other, and one, flown by Oblt. Karl Muller and with his engineer and gunner, Uffz. Johannes Korn came plummeting down to earth near Rye Hill (more or less where you find the two arches takeaway at junction 7 of the M25 if you are interested). Muller was able to parachute out of his fighter bomber and was taken Prisoner. He saw out the rest of the war in Canada. Sadly, Korn was not so lucky, and he died in the resulting crash. He was buried with full military honours at a local church and then his body was later reinterred at the German cemetery in Cannock Chase.

A couple of months later, we have a Dornier 17z; these bombers were used by the Luftwaffe in large numbers during the early part of the war. It was fast (for a bomber) and able to outmanoeuvre other aircraft making it much harder to hit, and carried a two thousand pound payload. It even had a nickname, 'the flying pencil' due to its incredibly narrow fuselage. This did not stop one being shot out of the sky on 15th November, 1940 whilst it was attempting a raid on London. The crashed aircraft landed near Latton Priory Farm, just north of Epping and all five crew on board died. Their names were Lt. Wagner, Fw. R. Grommer, Fw. A. Hans, Gefr. F. Heilig and Auffz. W. Hockendorf. As was the correct course of action, the bodies that were able to be recovered were given a proper burial.

The deaths continued – as they did around the world – and at 12.45am on the 8th December, 1940, witnesses watched a Junkers 88 go into a vertical dive, crashing to the ground by the Wake Arms Hotel in Epping after being brought down by anti-aircraft fire. The Ju88 had not released its four to five thousand pound bomb load and exploded on impact, immediately killing the four crew Uffr. M. Jappsen, Gefr. A. Dornauer, Fw. E. Leipold and Gefr. F. Weber.

Accidents and fatalities were not just limited to the German aircrews, as plenty of Allied pilots and support lost their lives as well. Putting stories behind these brave people on all sides is important when you can, and here is a bit about a 25-year-old pilot who died on the 30th August, 1940.

Feliks Gmur had been born in Poland on 6th November, 1914. He had flown with the Polish airforce as a fighter pilot and managed to escape shortly after the Nazi occupation, travelling through Romania and France and ending up in Britain where he joined up with the R.A.F. in early February 1940. He was taking part in a routine patrol on 30th August, 1940, flying his Hurricane R 4213 from his base at Stapleford Tawney when he encountered enemy aircraft. A dogfight ensued, but Sgt. Gmur's aircraft was damaged and he crashed near to Jacks Hatch, Epping Green, and did not survive.

The last fatality I am going to mention was over a year later, on 15th October 1941 and this tale of bravery that is one I have read of before, and even so, the level of forethought that must go into it still astonishes me. Pilot Officer Roger Hall

Atkinson of the 71st Eagle Squadron (the American contingent, before their country joined the war) had taken off from R.A.F. North Weald on a practice flight, but his Spitfire AD123 malfunctioned, and he knew he was going to have to attempt to bail out and allow the aircraft to crash. In order to avoid the town that he was airborne over, he managed to remain at the controls long enough to steer away from the populated areas with the aircraft going down in the Woodford part of Essex, but when he did try to escape, his parachute failed to open and he died. The young man from Illinois was only twenty years old.

So many fliers who were based at North Weald and Stapleford Tawney lost their lives during this time, please do visit the memorials to pay respects if you get the opportunity.

R.A.F. Chigwell

The airfield at North Weald was not the only R.A.F. base in the area, and I am not including the many towards London with Hornchurch, Fairlop and Chipping Ongar, but I refer to Chigwell.

Perhaps because it was never home to any runways, or launched any of the well-known aircraft associated with the Second World War means that many people do not even know it existed, but it had a very important function that deserves recognition.

If you are in the Chigwell area, and decide on visiting the David Lloyd Club, you will be playing tennis where the men and woman ate their meals, or the station administration was conducted. Walk a bit further towards the Roding Valley Meadows and you may come across concrete access roads. What did they lead to and what were they used for?

Even though the site did not house any aeroplanes, it played an important part in the protection of the skies over Great Britain, at least until 1943, as it was home to No. 4 Balloon Centre, part of the No. 30 (Balloon Barrage) Group. It was here that those giant methods of air defence were constructed, maintained and launched and whilst you may wonder what damage they could have done, let me hopefully educate you a bit about this protector up above.

There are conversations regarding barrage balloons in the parliamentary records well before the outbreak of the Second World War, in fact, there are references to the balloon training scheme at Cardington in mid - 1937, so air defence was something already being considered.

Construction began in Chigwell around this time for a training facility to cater for around seven-hundred balloon operators, and it was confirmed in March 1938 (so again, before the war was declared) that money had been put to one side to fund these projects. Recruitment to fill the centre - it was not known as R.A.F. Chigwell until April 1943 and was controlled at this point by the Auxiliary Air Force - started on the 16th May, 1938, and became operational as No. 4 Balloon Centre on the 4th August 1938 (*'Not all Airmen Fly'* by Jenny Filby & Geoff Clark).

 Run by the Royal Air Force, the men (and it was men to begin with, the Women's Auxiliary Air Force (W.A.A.F.) was formed in June 1939) would need to be educated on how to manage these hydrogen filled (the Hindenburg, anyone?) twenty-metre-long floating bombs. Once the W.A.A.F. started to prove their efficiency and ability to be substituted for R.A.F. men, the women gradually took on both the construction and operator roles of the balloons.

Each was made up of twenty-four different panels, rubberised Egyptian cotton, each panel coated on the outside with aluminium powder. The women would have to stand inside the balloon, sew them up, and then fill them to check the seams had been made airtight (although a certain amount of gas loss was expected). In most cases, the balloon would be attached to a winch on the back of a truck, and gradually filled with hydrogen to rise to a height of around five thousand feet.

What was the exact purpose of these? To force aircraft higher up and impede their efforts to practice precision bombing. Whilst they did not have much effect at all on the high-level attackers, it was the dive bombers that would get tangled up in the cables – of which some were actually weaponised and would cause even more damage than just the impact of an aircraft being hit by a trailing piece of thick steel (which would not be good in its own right).

There are cases in the papers, especially in early 1939 (so again, before 1st September 1939) of the general public being shown how these balloons would work - and also seeing the potential pitfalls, when a demonstration went awry after a surprise lightning strike hit the trailing metal cable and caused the balloon to crash to the ground in a ball of flames.

After a while, the balloons were not as efficient as the German bombing campaign became more sophisticated, but it was in 1944 (after they had moved away from Chigwell, stay with me here...) that they proved an effective weapon against the pilotless V1 flying bombs. The doodlebugs would get caught up in the cables and either trigger an explosion from the hydrogen gas, or their own guidance system would get confused and set the warhead off.

It was not just the balloons which appeared to be a bit dangerous however, the lorries which carried the winch used to hoist the structure into the air were cumbersome to drive and there were accounts of them losing control and crashing when driving through nearby Buckhurst Hill, specifically Palmerstone Road. I could not find any accounts of serious injuries however, well, nothing with a pulse, only inanimate objects like walls!

That is not to say that things did not go bang from time to time. In March of 1939, residents remembered seeing a balloon struck by lightning and bursting into flames, with a trailing metal cable earthing itself to the ground, they would have been an electrical conducting dream - which is why they were brought down whenever storms were forecast.

You may wonder why someone who is based in Chelmsford (another part of Essex for those who do not know the geography) is interested in this, but recently I found out an interesting fact about the hydrogen that was manufactured for these balloons. It transpires that from January 1942 to September 1944, the Corporation Gasworks at

Chelmsford was responsible for the production of a large percentage of the hydrogen produced for barrage balloons in general.

Many people (especially W.A.A.F.) trained at Chigwell to learn how to repair, and launch these relatively passive anti-aircraft measures, but it was not until April 1943, when the balloon unit left, and the site was taken over by the Mobile Signals Unit took over that it was designated as R.A.F. Chigwell.

These guys were not just learning how to operate radios, they had many different roles to play and the site was designed to help them learn all the things they would need as they were "mobile" (the title of the unit gives it away somewhat). They had to be taught how to deal with every single possible hurdle to get the communications where they needed to be, and that could include everything from setting up field kitchens, running radio masts to waterproofing vehicles to ford rivers!

Being able to get messages to other groups was intrinsic to success, and those sent here had a valuable job to do. The centre was so busy that some of the huge hangars (there had been three) that were originally used to house the giant balloons, were converted into accommodation for the thousands of people sent to Chigwell for training. All I need to mention is D-Day, and you will know that I am talking about a pretty critical event. This base trained units for that famous operation, set up the south coast radio scheme and also had people who had learned what to do upon setting foot on the shores of northern France just three days after the initial landings.

That is not to say that those based in the forest of Essex had no risk, the hangar which contained a lot of vehicles, equipment and records was attacked by the enemy on 18th February 1944, and most of it destroyed. It is somewhat fortunate it was not one of the other hangars that was full of recruits however, so fate was looking upon them favourably.

If you visit the area – and you can, as it is now the Roding valley nature reserve – you may find a stone that has the word "Intone" on it. For many years, this has confused historians and researchers as no Operation Intone is easily found, but the writers of the book 'Not All Airmen Fly' managed to get some information. By looking at the Commanding Officers log, they found an entry on the 11th July, 1943 which stated "11 vehicles despatched to port, no incidents, intone". It transpires it was to do with a Coastal Command Op involving 220 Squadron regarding anti-submarine duties in the Atlantic. In fact, they were the first squadron to use Flying Fortresses B-17 for this kind of work, they switched to the B-24 Liberator less than a year later (anyone who knows me will be able to tell you which of those two aircraft I prefer…).

What about ghosts, though? Well, the area does have a couple of stories, although I have never experienced anything there so cannot validate (or dispel), and I want to stress that these are second or third hand accounts. In 1968, a thirteen-year-old was making their way across the fields. R.A.F. Chigwell had been sold off four or five years previously, and the site was now owned and managed by Chigwell Urban District Council. They said they saw a man in a long overcoat, military type boots and whilst he was silent, he appeared to be screaming. The strangest thing was that he was totally transparent and the teenager could see the bushes behind him.

Rumours of someone being burned to death and haunting the area whilst serving during the war abound locally, but there is no historical validation for this.

The next recorded account was in 1993, a young woman walking her dog interacted with someone young and very "1940's-esque" in an old style R.A.F. uniform, when she turned around to see where he went, he had disappeared. There are no records of accidental deaths on the site from when it was a balloon centre or when it was anything else, however the authors of 'Not All Airmen Fly' did find an account of a suicide. Could this be the young man?

Lippitt's Hill

I mention this site in another chapter of this book, but it has such a varied history that it warrants being here as well.

This is also where I get to brag a bit, and also show that the old adage of "don't ask, don't get" is so very accurate, applies to this particular place. Prior to the outbreak of the Second World War, the area of Lippitt's Hill was predominantly fields, and in the area that we now see as the place where Metropolitan Police helicopters (amongst other things) are based and can be seen taking off from, was partly Piper's Farm and on the other side of the road, The Owl Public House (which is very nice if you are ever in the area and fancy a stop). In January 1940, with the threat of attack very real, anti-aircraft gun emplacement ZE7 Lippitt's Hill was opened. This was a heavy 'ack-ack' centre (ack-ack being the nickname for anti-aircraft guns for those who do not know) as opposed to some of the light ack-ack guns that were in place around the country. What I found interesting when researching for this part of the book was that the Ministry was happy for ack-ack (albeit lightweight guns) operators to be up to the age of fifty years old, and if they were former servicemen (at that point, it was men) then they could be up to fifty-five years old.

ZE7 was there to protect the eastern reaches of London from enemy aircraft, with four gun emplacements. You may have thought that it was like the clichéd "shooting fish in a barrel" to bring down low flying aircraft who had already navigated the barrage balloons that were helped into the air by nearby R.A.F. Chigwell, but not so. I found this description of the mathematical reasoning behind how many shells needed to be fired up into the air to stand a modicum of success of hitting anything by one Professor A.V. Hill in 1940:

"One cubic mile of space contains 5500000 cubic yards. The lethal zone of a 37-inch shell is only a few thousand yards and exists for only about one fiftieth of a second. In order to give a one-fiftieth chance of bringing down an enemy (plane) moving at 250 miles per hour and crossing a vertical rectangle ten miles wide and four miles high about 3000 37-inch shells would be required."

Did it work? This piece in the Essex Newsman Tuesday, 21ˢᵗ March 1944 would suggest it did.

"The barrage is so good that a pilot has to take his life in his hands to fly through it," said an expert. "No other country in the world has a rocket anti-aircraft barrage. Many people have mistaken the noise of a rocket shell for the bursting of a bomb, but a rocket can be recognised by its roar. It has no bang. * When a number of rockets are fired from one locality, each noise merges into one great roar, whereas, when a battery of guns is fired, each gun has a distinct bang."

So from January 1940 until the late summer 1942, the British were using the 3.7 inch guns, each would have a crew of around seven and fire between ten and twenty rounds per minute. After the British tenure at Lippitts Hill, the Americans of the 184ᵗʰ Anti-Aircraft Artillery battery came to defend London and were the first American crew to fire in defence of the city. There is a monument dedicated to them just on the perimeter of the base.

The amazing thing is that two of the four original guns still exist, although they are filled in with soil but you can still see the structure and where the original bunkers and ammunition depot were. I was lucky in that when I contacted the current occupants, The National Police Air Service (N.P.A.S.), and asked if I could go and have a look around, they were all too happy to oblige. A huge thanks to Bev and Zoe for their help and the tour, it is always amazing to touch history.

The next episode in the history of this site was its incarnation as a P.O.W. camp. In late 1944 (post

D-Day) it was redeveloped to take Axis prisoners until it was closed again in 1948 – many of the huts that were used for these prisoners of war are still there, and you can even see them if you use google earth to view the premises.

That was not the end to its use as a protector of the British skies, the next chapter in its story is to do with the Cold War. If you are ever lucky enough to visit the site, you will see a very odd greenish building behind wire, that looks suspiciously like a concrete fall-out type bunker (well it does to me anyway), and this is pretty much what it was. Built around 1951, this was one of the anti-aircraft operations rooms built to control the defence of the skies, post second World War. As with R.O.T.O.R. (the air defence radar system) this soon became obsolete with the advent of bombers which could fly higher and faster (and evade the chain home early warning systems), with more savvy guided missiles and constantly evolving technology. Saying that, the A.A.O.R. bunker at Lippitts Hill is still there and used by the Police Service for who knows what? (There were rumours of something to do with electrics and technology, but nobody seemed to know for sure and there was nobody around with a key unfortunately.)

The Police took over the camp in the late 50's, and a gun range amongst other training essentials was installed – in fact, Princes William and Harry were taken there around twenty- five years ago to learn how to shoot and also to evade kidnappers. There are many different branches of the Met based there, some quite secretive, but it is also the home of N.P.A.S. and the amazing helicopters which are there to look after us, even to this day.

Ghosts? I do not know, I was not there to investigate, but I was reliably informed that more than one person - and the witnesses range from police officers, to handymen, to even air crew – have seen a person walking around and heard them speaking German...one of the prisoners of war who came back?

Chapter 4 – Crime and Punishment

When you start to factor in the huge area that is classed as Epping Forest (semantics aside, yes, I do include the areas of Hainault and Waltham as part of this, but I am inherently lazy and do not want to keep repeating that). It is not surprising that crimes and unexplained deaths occurred within this area.

It was after I was asked to research the history of the larger area of Chigwell for the Celebrity episode of *Help! My House is Haunted* of which I was a part, that much of this information came to light and they asked me to investigate the practice of gibbeting as a method of punishment.

This was a type of criminal deterrent as opposed to punishment or execution and was an incredibly popular sentence in the 1740's and not officially stopped until 1834. If you put "Essex Gibbeting" into the search engine on the British Newspaper Archive, it produces nearly four thousand articles for the period 1700 to 1899, so it was definitely newsworthy. A person – and it was always male, the reason being that the bodies of females who had been condemned to death were highly sought after by those in the medical trade – was displayed in chains, hung invariably near to the point of their crime, and left there to rot. This practice had been further focussed on after the Murder Act of 1751 was passed. It specified that "In no case whatsoever shall the body of any murderer be suffered to be buried", meaning that if they were not to be dissected, they would be displayed in chains (or the more well-known cage that you can see in many museums).

The sight alone would have not been pleasant, and the smell would have been something else – even in 18th century England without any decent sanitation system.

Whilst the practice was going out of favour at the beginning of the 19th century, the last two took place only a few years before it was abolished. For those who are interested, the last two cases both took place in August 1832. The first - his execution was on the 3rd August, and the gibbet erected three days later – was William Jobling, a miner from Jarrow. He had begged for money from a local magistrate (Nicholas Fairles) and when the victim had refused, Jobling's friend Armstrong beat Fairles into unconsciousness. Despite the victim confirming that Jobling had not laid a finger on him, because they could not locate the former seaman Armstrong, the former was subsequently charged with murder when Fairles died from his injuries.

Just days later, the last ever gibbeting case took place in Leicester. James Cook, a bookbinder by trade was executed for the murder of a man to whom he was indebted, John Paas, on the 10th August 1832, and subsequently displayed in chains. Although it has to be said that locals demanded it was taken down after a very short while as the stench became unbearable to them.

There are a couple of specific cases which jump out when looking at a connection with the forest area, those of you with a delicate composition may wish to look away now…

Searching newspaper reports of the day, there are a couple of accounts which are worth highlighting as they took place in the area that we are focussed on. On the 28th March, 1752, murderers John Swann and Elizabeth Jeffries were hanged at the six mile marker in Epping Forest. Swann is reported to have taken nearly fifteen minutes to die, struggling desperately for air at the end of the rope, and his accomplice was so distraught she passed out more than once on the journey from the prison in Chelmsford to her death. The whole spectacle was designed to dissuade people from committing similar crimes, with the procession of over twenty-five miles taking the pair through Essex villages and towns like Ingatestone, Brentwood, Romford and Ilford – the judge also specified that Elizabeth would be sat on her coffin in a cart, whereas Swann would be dragged on a sled with no comfort whatsoever.

What had they done? On the face of it, it was a pretty horrible crime. She had been living with her Uncle Joseph in Walthamstow. He had "adopted" her from his brother when she was about five years old to provide her with the kind of life that her birth father could not. He was a benevolent relative and by all the witness statements heard in court, a kind and generous man. What could have possibly caused Elizabeth to persuade Swann - who worked for Jeffries - to shoot him dead on the 3rd July, 1751, and run off with his master's niece after stealing from her Uncle? To all observers of the case, it was pretty obvious that they had taken advantage of a gentle older man and murdered him in cold blood to gain financially. As with so many cases, there was an awful lot more to it if you dig further, and there is also the question as to whether Elizabeth was actually the victim rather than a killer.

I mentioned earlier in the last paragraph that Elizabeth had been made part of his household by her uncle at the age of 5; some of her statements in court seem to contradict this compassionate and generous gesture. It was more the case that she was taken by him and that it was not her birth father's choice. Once she reached around the age of fifteen the abuse began. Her uncle would repeatedly rape her, and she stated she had suffered at least two miscarriages that she knew of. Few newspapers seemed to report this, the *Manchester Mercury on 24th March 1752* being one.

Miss Jeffries has further confessed, That her Uncle took her from her Father when she was Five Years old; and that, when she was Sixteen, her said Uncle debauched her: That she lived in a continual State of Incest with him (having had two Miscarriages by him) till about a Year before his Death, when he slighted her in favour of another Woman. His repeated Neglects of her, and his threatening to alter his Will, which she knew had been made entirely in her Favour, were the Motives that induced her to perpetrate the Murder; for which she is sentenced to die.

So, it appears from this, that her kindly and benign Uncle was actually a sexual predator and threatened to remove her from his will and leave her destitute if she was not willing to allow him to assault her on a regular basis. Maybe once she had reached around twenty years old, she was not as attractive to him anymore and it does make you wonder who the new woman was - or maybe that should read girl?

Her body was given back to her family for interment, and quietly buried at St. Saviours Church in Southwark, whereas Swann's remains were placed in chains and moved to be displayed outside The Bald Faced Stag pub in Buckhurst Hill (always written as Buckets Hill in accounts of the time) as this was a drinking establishment that his master had previously frequented. It is quite sad how many accounts of this quite famous killing at the time make no mention of the abuse that Elizabeth suffered, and just paint her as a money-hungry harlot rather than the victim that some of this evidence shows her as.

The other case I want to mention is that of Matthew Snatt, he had been a baker based at Brook Street in Holborn (London), when on the 21st March, 1757, he violently robbed the Norwich Mail and went on the run. He was apprehended and brought to trial but maintained his innocence. A news report from the July hearings stated that the Lord Chief Justice Mansfield who was overseeing the case said that they should take Snatt away and press him with weights until he changed his plea to guilty. I can honestly say I did not expect to see this method of torture used in 18th century Britain. He was then moved to Chelmsford where he was found guilty at the Assizes there, and his death sentence was passed, but this was not the only fate that was to befall him. The Judge also stated his body should be displayed in chains in Leytonstone where he had committed the crime. He was hanged at Chelmsford Prison on 12th August, 1757, and the

next day, his gibbet was erected outside The Bald
Faced Stag pub in Buckhurst Hill - the same place
as John Swann, five years earlier.

This pub is still there, although it has changed a
bit from the original building that dated back to at
least 1725, but was rebuilt in 1937 after being
badly damaged by fire the year before. There is
nothing suspicious linked to the incident, but
during the demolition and subsequent renovation,
workmen are said to have discovered three very
old pistols bricked up in the fireplace, and many
believed they matched the description of those
carried by the infamous Highwayman Dick Turpin.
Whether they were in fact the property of the
criminal himself is open for debate, but we do
know that he had strong links to the area of
Buckhurst Hill, so may have hidden them there.

I mentioned in the myths and legends chapter
about the treatment that Turpin meted out to the
old lady whose backside he held onto the hot
grate until she said where her money was hidden.
This took place at an old farmhouse on Traps Hill
in Loughton. There is a ghost story attached to
this horrific assault, which I am sure that you
would like to hear. According to folklore, three
times a year, Turpin is seen riding down the hill at
speed upon his famous horse, Black Bess, with a
look of terror on his face. He is said to be
watching out for the victim of this event as she
hides by the old lime tree on her property, set to
pounce onto the back of Bess and force Turpin to
retrieve her stolen gold.

I like the thought of ethereal justice, and someone
who could not possibly have fought against Turpin
in life, getting her revenge in death.

Another case connected with the area which always intrigues those who do a search for interesting stories is that of poor Emma Jane Heywood (also known as Giles). On the 27th July, 1895, Emma Jane was found dead in a field on the grounds of Grange Farm, Chigwell. She had been living with William Pond for over two years, although "living" is perhaps not the right word to use, they were roaming the countryside, picking up work where they could – having met reportedly whilst pea picking in nearby Romford – and bedding down wherever there was shelter. On the Saturday night before she was discovered, they had been seen drinking extensively and smoking a clay pipe after failing to secure any work. The mystery surrounding her arose when her death had been alerted to the police, but she showed signs of having drowned - no other injuries were apparent on her body at all, apart from some scratches to her right knee. How could she have drowned when there was no water nearby? What else could have happened? The relatively new science of post-mortems were coming to the fore, and during the Coroner's hearing, the divisional surgeon of the police, Dr. A. Ambrose confirmed that even he thought on first sight of the body, death from water was the obvious cause, due to foam around her mouth, but after examining the body and looking at the organs it was quite obvious that poor Emma Jane was an alcoholic and that her death had been due to apoplexy and nothing more sinister.

Basically, she drowned in her own vomit.

Her partner, William, confirmed that she was paralytically drunk on the day in question, and that he was trying to drag her to a place of safety to let her sleep it off, which he thought he had done. In her stupor she must have wandered off, passed out and been sick whilst unconscious which gave the illusion of drowning to a non-medically trained observer. Whilst finding out that the death was from natural causes and no nastiness at play, it does make you wonder how a twenty-eight year old woman could get to this stage in life? Had she always led a nomadic lifestyle? We know that the workhouses of the time had vagrant units which people who traipsed the countryside looking for odd jobs to pay for their next meal (or drink) could stay at for a short period of time, so this was not unheard of, but how did Emma Jane end up like this?

She was born Emma Janes Eaves in Darsham, Suffolk, in the last few months of 1866 to what appears to have been quite a low-income family. The next time she appears on the census records is in 1881 when she is working for the Jeacock family as a domestic servant and living at The Limes, Yoxford. One of the stories that the courts heard was that she had been seduced by an older gentleman with money when she was in the employ of a well to do family, and we find her in 1883, marrying Henry Giles. Where we can draw a definite link to her tale of being enchanted by this older man is that her first husband was born in 1846, and was the son of Sophia Giles - who is named as being a visitor to the Jeacock family on the 1881 census records. So here we have a man who is nearly twenty years her senior, and obviously not from the same kind of background as she was. She became Mrs. Giles in 1883, and in 1885 Henry Jnr. was born, and around a year later another son, Sidney. The next we hear of her is in 1891 when she was widowed, residing in Bethnal Green and according to the records "living off her own means". So, we can quite safely assume that Henry had died at some point in the previous five years. Fast forward another two years and she got married again to a man by the name of Joseph Haywood (sometimes spelled Heywood it appears). It must have been around this time that she met William Pond as they had been together for a couple of years when she died, but what is even more tragic is that when asked about her sons by people, she replied that she did not know where they were. One theory I did have for her sudden change in personality, going from relative financial security to living off the land and turning to drink was that she suffered another bereavement, possibly that of a child. There is one that may fit listed on the records, an Edmund Vaughan Heywood, the maiden name of his mother is unlisted but he was born in the third quarter of 1893 in Fulham and died in early 1894 (Emma Jane married Joseph in the first quarter of 1893).

It is quite sad to read about this young woman's decline, she was only twenty-eight years old when she died, not knowing what had happened to her sons and choking in a field miles from where she was from. Whatever was the reason for leaving the security of a home and marriage was, it is definitely a tragic story and I hope she is at rest now.

That is not to say that crime was (and is) not common in the forest, with all those miles of ground to commit any kind of felony, it is not surprising that there are scores of incidents we can talk about, so I am going to mention just four more.

On June 9th, 1878, Charles and Esther Revell were having a meal with her mother, as was common for the young couple (he was only twenty-five years old). They were having a disagreement, primarily over some money that Esther had loaned to her husband and wanted back as she knew he would go and spend it on alcohol (the sum was three shillings). In anger, Charles stormed out of the house and Esther followed, whether to placate him or in determination to retrieve her money, nobody truly knows, but she was never seen again as her body was found near to Lippitt's Hill with her throat cut. Not unsurprisingly, suspicion soon fell upon her spouse and he was arrested not long after, and sentenced to be hanged for the offence. On the 29th July, 1878, he was executed by William Marwood at Springfield Gaol (Chelmsford), and by all accounts was incredibly penitent for what he had done. He did admit to what he had done to twenty-two-year-old Esther, trying to perhaps find reason in his actions by saying it was due to jealousy and that he had struck her first.

Certainly, the next case has elements of the green eyed monster in it as well, or at least that is what one of the participants blamed his actions on. On the 17th May, 1922, fifty-four year old George Stanley Grimshaw, a decorator living in Walthamstow, was found dying from severe head injuries in the Highams Park area of Epping Forest. He lost his life shortly after in Whitcross Hospital and a murder investigation was started.

It did not take the police long to find out that Grimshaw had been meeting up with a young waitress from the Braintree area called Elsie (who was twenty-two years old) and they had been conducting an affair. It seems that Elsie was actually married to William Yeldham, and he had followed her after a huge row and found her sitting with Grimshaw. This was more than her husband could apparently cope with and he launched a frenzied attack on the older man, beating him repeatedly around the head. When Yeldham was sure he had completed the task, he ordered his young wife to steal whatever they could from Grimshaw – a watch and around £15 in cash – and leave. Although passers-by found Grimshaw, and had him conveyed to hospital, he could not be saved, and so Mr. and Mrs. Yeldham were tried in court on murder charges. In the August of 1922, William's mother wrote an impassioned letter to the Home Secretary begging for his death sentence to be changed, explaining that there was a history of mental illness in the male line and that his father had died in an asylum, so it was obvious that her son had not known what he was doing and had surely been mentally incapacitated at the time. It seems that there was no mood for leniency in this case, and he was hanged by John Ellis in H.M.P. Pentonville on 5th September 1922, whilst expressing sympathy for Mrs. Grimshaw in respect of her philandering husband but none for the man he had killed.

Elsie was reprieved, but this piece of correspondence in the Woman's Leader dated 8th September, 1922 does somewhat suggest that the trial was conducted unfairly:

ELSIE YELDHAM.

MADAM,—We desire in the first place to thank those friends who helped by subscription and sympathy in the case of Mrs. Yeldham.

As your readers know, the Lord Chief 'Justice dismissed the appeal, though admitting that " it was unfortunate " that she had not been informed that she had a right to make a statement. The Home Office, however, the next day, reprieved Mrs. Yeldham.

We cannot but feel that it is a grave scandal that a woman should be tried and sentenced to death without being defended by counsel, and without even being informed that she had the right to give evidence on her own behalf, and to address the jury ; and we feel that the defence, and the publicity given to the matter did much to prevent the death sentence being actually enforced.

The subscriptions, however, have not been sufficient to cover the full expenses of the defence, which amount to £68. We are therefore—though reluctantly—asking for further donations.

A. SUSAN LAWRENCE.
MADELEINE J. SYMONS.

Not all murders are solved however, and the following is one such case.

It was 9th November, 1946 and newly demobbed R.A.F. man, Kenneth Dolden had driven to the forest - Fairmead Bottom area - with his fiancée, twenty-two year old school teacher, Jacinth Bland after a night of dancing and celebrating their forthcoming wedding. They were sitting in the back of Kenneth's car, when a masked man banged on the door. As Dolden got out to remonstrate with him, the man opened fire on Jacinth's fiancé and fired three shots point-blank range into his torso. The shooter then ran off into the forest, leaving a terrified Jacinth to try and find help for her bleeding partner. The victim did not die straight away and was able to give a statement to the police, confirming that he had no idea who the gunman was, and that he had never seen him before. It must have been utterly terrifying for poor Jacinth, watching the man she was due to marry gunned down in cold blood and for absolutely no reason whatsoever. The traditional lines of enquiry followed, searching for any enemies. Could it have been a case of mistaken identity? Was it a peeping Tom? To this day, the case is still unsolved and no-one knows why poor young military man, Kenneth Dolden was shot in Epping Forest.

This last case I discovered has me asking quite a few questions, and should the police at the time have had access to the computer systems we have, they may have drawn similar conclusions to me.

On the 5th August, 1895 a young lad was hunting for blackberries in the forest when he discovered a brown paper parcel partially hidden in the bushes. Upon opening it, he found the body of a fully developed baby boy, and medical professionals later said the child was at least a week old, but death had been caused quite obviously by murder – he had been strangled by a piece of tape wrapped tightly around his throat. That alone is horrible to think of, and for the poor kid who discovered it, but it made me wonder about one of the most famous child killers of that time, Amelia Dyer. She was what is known as a "baby farmer", someone who is paid to take in children of mothers who cannot cope and do not want to rely on somewhere like a children's home or orphanage. Many of these baby farmers did not take care of the children under their charge, and worked out how to make money – by killing them. Whilst Dyer was certainly not the only one, she was caught out in March, 1896 and executed on 10th June of the same year after a bargeman discovered the body of a young child - that of Helena Fry - in the Thames, wrapped in brown paper with a piece of tape wound to the point of asphyxiation around her neck. In fact, when Dyer was caught, she was almost proud of her trademark tape, and estimates believe that rather than just the three poor souls she was executed for, that there were hundreds.

Is the baby in the woods one of them?

Chapter Five – Tragedy

Unsurprisingly, a huge area like Epping Forest has seen its fair share of tragedies, and it was quite difficult deciding which stories I would include in this chapter as opposed to others. For example, the 'suicides' of people like William Barnes and William Silwood - and if you wonder why I have put that word in inverted commas, read the chapter that I wrote about what happened to them, I do not believe they took their own lives - were both linked to the legend of the suicide pond as well as being incredibly sad events. The many murders that took place over the years, the aircraft crashes during and after the Second World War…all of these are awful events that we should remember, but I chose to include them in more bespoke chapters and focus this one on slightly different misfortunes.

Again, it was when I was researching for the celebrity episode of *Help!My House is Haunted* based in Chigwell that I came across this case.

On the 22nd July, 1891, a commercial traveller who is documented as being Charles Hicks found a distraught woman by the name of Mary Jane Heathcote. She was making a moaning noise and swaying in shock on the balcony of the Royal Forest Hotel in Chingford (more about this place in Chapter 10, Buildings). Obviously distraught and needing some kind of assistance – he noticed she was soaking wet, and he noted it had not been raining - he asked the young woman what was troubling her. She told him quite bluntly that she had murdered her two children and wanted to be taken to the local police station.

She then spoke with the Sergeant at Chingford police station and began to explain that she was married to a very decent man by the name of Joseph Heathcote, a hatter's salesman, and had been living at 66, Kynaston Road in Stoke Newington with their two daughters, five-year-old Florence (known as Florrie) and three-year-old Emily (known as Cissy). A few months beforehand, the three of them had suffered badly with influenza but the girls had not recovered very well and she was terrified they were not going to be healthy ever again, and what would happen if she were to die and leave them motherless? What sort of life would her daughters have if they were permanently disabled by this illness? Whilst her testimony did not mention the workhouse, the fear of that being Florrie and Cissy's future would have been very real due to the stigma that it produced.

She had travelled the seven miles from Stoke Newington, alternating between her children walking unaided and carrying them when they were tired. Once they reached the forest, she laid them down in the stream which ran behind the hotel, subsequently placing herself on top of them, her plan to take both their lives and hers. She had a note on her person which was intended as a suicide letter.

Oh, my dear husband, I cannot live any longer. All is against us, but I would face it all if the children were well, but they never will be again. I have prayed for them day and night, but no change bee come. We must all die together, for illness means ruin to us all. Ever since I went home I have noticed a change in everybody to me, which I cannot bear. Oh, how I long to be at rest, for this is awful. Lay me with my darlings.

When the search party found Florrie and Cissy, they were judged to be well fed, dressed adequately and had pebbles in their pockets to weigh them down. A neighbour in their home confirmed she was a good mother but she truly believed as a concerned citizen, that it was Mary Jane's worries of leaving the children with only one parent to care for them, and a certain amount of religious zealousness caused her breakdown.

"Oh, my dear husband, I cannot live longer; I would face it all if the children were well, but they never will be again. I have prayed for them day and night, but no change has come; we must all die together, for illness means ruin to us all. Ever since we went home there has been a change in everybody to me that I cannot bear. Oh, how I long to be at rest, for this is awful; lay me with my darlings, the sinner and the sinned against, but not on purpose, for no mother ever loved her children more than I have; they were all I have lived for. Good-bye, and may God have mercy on us all"

The hearing at the Old Bailey on 14th September, 1891 confirmed that she was not of sound mind, in fact, the witness statement by the medical officer of Holloway Gaol, Philip Francis Gilbert was quite unequivocal:

"I have kept careful observation of the prisoner since her admission there—she has been under constant watching—when I first saw her she was of unsound mind, suffering from melancholia—

although she is now better, I still think that she is not responsible—beyond the melancholia she has had two almost maniacal attacks while in the prison—attacks of acute mania"

Whilst she was found guilty of murder, she was also deemed not compos-mentis as mentioned in the court case and was to be detained at her Majesty's pleasure. This is where most newspaper coverage of her case ends, we know that she was going to be in what you could describe as the mental health wing of Holloway Prison, but that was the last we hear of her.

I was interested to find out what happened to Mary Jane, and to see if she managed to have a future and forgive herself for what she did. Her husband, it seems, moved to Oregon, America in 1900, and Mary Jane followed on 15th May, 1914 aboard the R.M.S. Empress of Ireland, departing Liverpool, her last address documented as being with her sister in Swindon. She arrived in Quebec on the 22nd May, 1914, and then boarded the S.S. Princess Charlotte, landing in Seattle a week later. I would say she was glad that she had travelled the dates she did, as the Empress of Ireland started its journey back from Quebec to Liverpool six days later but sank after colliding with the S.S. Storstad, a Norwegian cargo ship. The loss of life was horrendous, over a thousand people died including over one hundred and thirty children.

S.S. Storsted after her collision with R.M.S. Empress of Ireland

The Grim Reaper was to follow Mary Jane when Joseph, the husband who seems to have stood by her (and paid for her passage to the United States) died on 4th October, 1917. To some, the fact that she re-married two years later to Thomas Bathe may seem mercenary, but she had no trade other than housewife. Bathe was quite a bit older than Mary Jane, and he died in the June of 1925. She then married William Steele ten months later, they were married up until her death on the 12th January, 1942. William passed away just months later.

There is a strong belief that if it is not your time, you will cheat death, which Mary Jane seems to have done more than once, what with not receiving a death penalty after the murder of her children (having been deemed not of sound mind), travelling on a ship that just a week later sank with the loss of nearly seventy percent of those on board and outliving two husbands – either she was cursed to watch people die around her or she had a very strong guardian angel watching over her every move.

Once you start looking into cases of those who have suffered, and with such a huge area to cover, there are sadly many that you could write about, and I have had to restrict my reporting to a paltry few.

Murder suicide is always one that hits you in the soul, and on the 4th August, 1900 farm hands were working the land near High Beech, when under a "shock" of wheat they found two bodies, both of whom had gunshot wounds and were deceased.

Upon further investigation, they were identified as forty-five-year-old Auguste Mottlau and twenty-year-old Olga Schmitt, both recent immigrants from Denmark and worked together. Upon reading their suicide note it became clear that they had been having an affair (Mottlau was married) and felt that this was the only way of getting forgiveness - in life and in death.

I am sure it was their families, and the poor workers who found them, that suffered the most with that decision, but the tragic side for me is that they were new to the country and could not carry on the way they were.

The world wars always produce horrible accounts, and sadly many have been forgotten as they were never documented properly due to secrecy and the worry that spies would convey back to the enemy the location of the hits – not to mention wanting to convince the British public that it was not as bad as they thought, 'bulldog spirit' and all that.

Looking at evacuation plans now, some of the areas that people were moved to that were deemed safe seems laughable, but relocated they were, and in late 1939, Spriggs Oak House, owned by Mr. W. F. Trent was converted into a home for expectant mothers – the majority being from East London. I am guessing that nobody foresaw this beautiful Georgian property being in the line of fire, but on the 9th October, 1940 at 8:05pm, a bomb hit it, killing eight pregnant women and injuring at least fourteen more – the only reason the death and injury toll was not higher is said to be due to Clark Gable and Joan Crawford, as many had gone to the local cinema to watch their most recent film.

The women were Bertha Fleischman (twenty-five), Adela Franks (twenty-eight), Lily Sly (twenty-nine), Ellen Campbell (twenty-four), Violet Buckle (nineteen), Rose Revenski (thirty-four), May Banks (thirty) and Elizabeth Louisa Smith (twenty-two) - and keep in mind, all were pregnant.

I wonder how many of the people who live in the beautiful apartments that now occupy Spriggs Oak House know of what happened there back in 1940? It probably does not help that the bomb is not mentioned on the bombsight.org map, which shows the sites of all explosives dropped from 7th October 1940 to 6th June, 1941. There is a memorial plaque in Epping to these women, and although the town itself avoided any major loss compared to nearby Chigwell, Loughton and Buckhurst Hill, it still puzzles me that it is not widely known.

The Second World War was responsible for a lot of pain and hurt for many civilians all round the world, but this next account is an incident that people should know about.

Take yourself back to the London Blitz, the bombardment has been going on since September 1940 and it is now the 19th April, 1941. The war has been going on since September 1939, but over the last six months or so, civilians have seen bombs being dropped on cities like London and its surrounding areas at a rate never experienced before. I guess the trick was to try and carry on as normally as possible, which is why on that Saturday night, the regulars of the Prince of Wales pub, Manor Road, Chigwell were enjoying a pint and a game of darts, blissfully unaware of what was about to happen.

To us now, Chigwell is part of Greater London, however back in 1941 it was Essex, but with hindsight, people may have known how dangerous it was going to be, after all, between the periods of September 1944 and March 1945, the area had nine V2 rockets land there, the second highest in the whole of Essex (the dubious title of the most heavily bombed area in that capacity goes to Hornchurch, which did have an incredibly successful forward fighter base, so was a target).

Parachute mines had been used to disrupt naval shipping from early in the war, dropped from aircraft into the water, they would wait to detonate after the detection of a magnetic field would cause detonation (unlike a depth charge for instance, that would go off automatically). It is said that Hermann Goring began using these in the early stages of the Blitz - either to target London docks or in a fit of pique, no-one really knows – there were a couple of types, weighing upwards of five-hundred kilograms and the smallest being four inches short of six foot. They would be released from the aircraft with a parachute attached and travelling at around forty miles per hour. Once they hit the ground, there was a timer delay of twenty-five seconds before explosion, the sound of the parachute flapping must have been really confusing just before it blew up.

It was one of these that landed on the Prince of Wales pub on that Saturday night, ending in a matter of seconds the lives of at least forty people, not only that, destroying the futures of many more when their loved ones were killed by the explosion. The venue itself was totally destroyed and did not open for eight years due to the damage. As with so many pubs, it shut permanently in the 1990's, and was ripped down and replaced by apartments where you can find a small memorial plaque outside to those that lost their lives on that night.

Looking through the list of the deceased via the Commonwealth War Graves Commission, it makes for very sad reading, a mixture of ages ranging from early fifties to mid-twenties. Royal Observer Corps like Gordon Mackie who was only thirty-eight years old, Police Officers Benjamin Wathen (twenty- nine) and Leonard Ives (thirty-two), Leading Fireman Albert Mason who was forty, twenty-nine-year-old Frederick Carter who was a member of the Home Guard, William S. Fyfe, who at fifty-three had seen service with the Royal Engineers in the First World War and was helping the war effort by working with the Home Guard.

These and many more brave people perished in the explosion and resulting collapse of the pub, one of many tragic stories worldwide from that time, but also something that many have forgotten about.

Some of you may wonder why I am talking about such horrible events in this chapter, it is not to glorify the awfulness in any way or for people to go running off to the woods with Ouija board in hand and attempt to contact any of these poor souls. My reason for writing about them is respect, pure and simple, to offer in my own way, condolences to the families who I am sure still remember these relatives with a mixture of sadness and smiles. So, if you do ever go and investigate these areas, and any of these names or references come through, be kind, gracious and considerate, there are still many alive today who are descended from these victims.

Teenagers all over have always vied for independence and for those of us who are parents, it is an incredibly fine line between allowing them that freedom whilst still watching over them whilst they learn how to stay as safe as possible.

Sadly, it can sometimes go horribly wrong, as in the tragic case of fifteen year old Marion Hartley.

By all accounts, this resident of Forest Glade in Chingford was a popular girl, and on the evening of the 23rd July, 1966 she had persuaded her parents to let her go to a dance at the nearby Woodford Memorial Home. After leaving her friend shortly before midnight to go their own short ways back to their houses, she was snatched by twenty year old Irishman Joseph Kiely, assaulted and strangled. A neighbour had heard a commotion, and looking out of his window, saw someone half-carrying and half-dragging a body into the bushes and called the Police. It did not take long for the investigators to find Kiely, as his wallet and betting slips had been left by the body of poor Marion, and they discovered him messy and dishevelled, which he blamed on the fact he had been sleeping rough and was of no fixed abode. When the leading police officer told him that they intended to charge him with the murder of Marion, his reply was *'I was very drunk and I did not know what I was doing.'*

Kiely had come to England from Dublin earlier in the month of July. Somehow, despite being unemployed he had imbibed at least twelve pints of beer at a Walthamstow pub – according to the landlord - before attacking the poor girl and killing her.

Originally, he was charged with murder, and when the trial was held (the records are still closed until at least 2052), his defence team pushed for a much lesser charge of manslaughter, with medical evidence from Brixton Prison confirming that he was illiterate and also had the mental age of a nine-year-old, so diminished responsibility was a valid reason to accept the reduction of sentence. The judge awarded a fifteen-year term of imprisonment, which according to reports I have read, Kiely served only eight before he was released and went back to Ireland where by all accounts, he is very much a social pariah that nobody wants to associate with.

Just one more awful tragedy to add to the soil of Epping Forest and the souls for whom it is their resting place.

I was not sure where to include this next few thousand words, it could have gone in quite a few of the chapters, but to balance things out (and to illustrate that maybe this was also tragic) I have included it here.

The Royal Gunpowder Mills of Waltham Abbey.

Whilst the site today is small in comparison to what it once was (a quick look at the archives available at https://www.wargm.org/archive_viewer/ will give you a better idea as to the size of the place in its heyday), it is still a large complex of buildings, many of which you can tell their 19th century origins from.

There was a fulling mill on the site back in 1590, but the manufacture of gun powder is believed to have begun at Waltham Abbey around 1665, and it was also the site of the first recorded deaths due to a powder mill (where the gunpowder is made from charcoal, saltpetre and sulphur) of Thomas Guttridge and Edward Simons. Making this explosive was incredibly risky, as the merest spark could ignite the powder, and that could even include a person's shoe causing friction with a stone floor.   Thomas was buried on the 4th October that year, and Edward the 5th October.

I could probably fill an entire chapter (even a book) on the mills at Waltham Abbey. A quick glance through newspaper articles from the mid-1700s onwards produces a glut of articles talking about explosions, death and injuries that were resultant from the making of firstly gunpowder, then gun cotton, cordite and even R.D.X. (which for the aviation enthusiasts amongst you will know it was used in the infamous bouncing bombs invented by Barnes Wallis and dropped by the Dambusters).

To give you some idea as to how dangerous this factory was, I will start with 27th November 1811. There are very precarious elements to gunpowder production, and it is why the separate stages are kept apart from each other to try and reduce the risk of a huge accident – something that did not work in 1811.

The reports of the time say that the blast originated in the press house (where the powder was pressed into cakes), but this caused a chain reaction with further detonations of the corning house (where the pressed powder was broken up into grains) and some of the other buildings. What is even more indicative of the force of the blast was that houses as far away as Stepney and Blackheath heard the noise and had windows shattered as a result. At least eight men lost their lives and most ominously, one newspaper report states " *The adjoining river, had been drawn for the dead bodies, but only three of them, and a part of one, had been found." (Bury and Norwich Post - Wednesday 04 December 1811).* I know that we are keen to pay tribute to ammunition workers who risked their lives in the first and second world war, but I believe that we should honour these men as well; Parker, Stevens, Grapes, Goats, Belcher, Wakeling, Chappel and Wilsher – all died due to the danger of producing something which was designed to kill, especially in 1811. What makes this even more tragic is that one of the men had seven children, another one was expecting a new baby and his poor wife miscarried when she heard the news.

It would not be difficult to comprehend that this was not the last big workplace related disaster to hit the mills, whilst they may have employed what we would see as rudimentary safety procedures by 21st century standard, they still tried. There would be a changing area for clothes away from the volatile materials they were working with, workers would be fined if they were found with even a stone in the sole of their shoe, and the different buildings were constructed apart from each other, with a huge brick buttress measuring twenty feet in height, fifteen feet in depth and around thirty feet long to act as a blast defence to stop any fire or explosion causing a chain reaction in neighbouring departments.

On the 13th April, 1843, this did not stop another big loss of life. Four separate huts - I say huts, but these constructions were eighty foot long, thirty foot or so wide and were made of wood with slate roofs and would be used for the process of corning, pressing, washing or glazing. At about 3.05pm on that day, the first of the buildings – the corning house – blew up, then literally moments later, a second explosion occurred as a pressing house and washing house exploded. This was not the end of the destruction however, as two-hundred yards from the first blast, another corning house went up and then the last to go was a second press and wash house. These were all separated from each other as advised, and the thick stone wall that was meant to stop fire progressing did not seem to help. Seven poor men lost their lives, and the circumstances were not peaceful nor in any way romantic. Five of them were blown to actual pieces clear across the river, one was found in the smoking ruins of his former workplace and the other was found intact but again, the power of the explosion had thrown him across the river.

The only reason the death toll was not considerably higher was that the buildings which went in the third and fourth blasts were unoccupied as they were being renovated, if not, there would have been an even greater loss of life.

Not that those who did perish should be forgotten. John Newland, John Dudley, James Luck, Samuel Brown, James Cole…Thomas Sadd was the master worker and Edward Essex was sixty-eight years old and had worked at the mills for over fifty years. In a cynical but realistic way, Edward had apparently said that he knew that being killed in an accident at his work was the way he would go, almost prophetic in a sense.

It also affected those living nearby. A report in Essex Herald - Tuesday 18 April 1843 said:

An aged female, named Bates, who resides in cottage about half mile distant from the scene of the catastrophe, was affected in the same way. She instantly exclaimed that it was one of the corning-houses that had exploded. The fatal sound was not new to her, as her husband was severely injured by like calamity some forty years ago and has ever since been considerately employed the government where the duty is less laborious.

Anyone within a good five-mile radius (a witness in Hoddesdon said it sounded like thunder) would have heard the noise and possibly felt the shock of the blast. Had they visited the site just after, they would have seen huge timbers smouldering and half buried in the marshland, buildings totally levelled, ripped clothing scattered high into the trees and people frantically searching for missing colleagues.

It must have been horrific.

You may wonder why this place interests me. Apart from its history, I had a very strange experience there back in 2014 in the middle of the day. We had taken our two sons out for a bit of family time, they were five and one, and we thought that the older of the two would enjoy learning about the science side of explosives and seeing the history of bombs and such. The younger one was totally oblivious so I took him for a stroll along the waterway which was used to power the mills and transport the various produce to different parts of the country. Across from where I stood was a long row of prefab type buildings, they looked pretty run down and there were signs everywhere saying "do not enter". I was looking at them wondering what they had been when I saw very clearly a woman walk past the window, but inside the derelict edifice, she did not seem to notice me but was wearing a type of cloth hat. I thought it strange that someone was inside what looked to me, as quite a dangerous falling-down wreck, and even more so without a hard hat, but I chalked it up to "nowt as queer as folk" and went back to join my husband and eldest son. It was only afterwards when I was looking up some information to do with the mills that I found out who had worked in these buildings. It was women building munitions for the First World War.

Women workers operating the guncotton pulping plant Royal Gunpowder Factory, Waltham Abbey, 1917.

https://www.nationalarchives.gov.uk/doc/open-government-licence/version/2/ taken from the Royal Gunpowder Mills website

From that discovery onwards, I have wanted to get back into this place and conduct a more focussed investigation, and I got the chance to have a try with the great guys from Ghost Hunt U.K. in January 2023. Whilst we were limited on where we could go with it being a public investigation (sadly no W.W.1 munition huts included), there were definitely some interesting things going on. Table tipping where the table glided across the floor as though it was on runners, a glow stick which was hanging from the ceiling started swinging for absolutely no reason whatsoever (Mark and Emily, thanks for showing me that video) but it was some of the spirit box activity that surprised me. Whilst in the museum, I had my eyes closed and the P.S.B-7 blasting into my ears. It was running backwards and at a rate of around 250 on AM, yet I was getting full, legible sentences. When I do an Estes type experiment, I tend to blurt out whatever I hear, especially as I do not know what questions other people are asking. I remember saying "make an appointment" and then shortly after, "she's gone". At the time it made no sense to me whatsoever, but one of the G.H.U.K. team came up to me and asked how I knew – for privacy, I am not mentioning her name, but this is how our conversation went:

"How did I know what?"

"What had been said to me a week or so ago on an investigation."

Me, still none the wiser "what was said to you?" and here is the kicker:

"Make an appointment, you said those exact words when I was standing near you and as I walked away you said, she's gone...how did you know?" I had to admit I had no clue she was there, I certainly did not know what had been said to her before and I did not see her walk away.

Messages will always come through, in one way or another.

Any event where someone has lost their life is a tragedy, but with this one I was contemplating whether it should go in the crime chapter I had written, or in here as some of the circumstances surrounding it do seem to be quite an unfortunate culmination of events over a period of years.

When I was recently at The National Archives (which for a research junkie like me is the equivalent to visiting Nirvana, the mother ship finally called me home) I found the case of Albert Bartlett who on the 19th October, 1920 had murdered Caroline Jervis. On the face of it, it seemed like quite a basic case and then I started reading more.

The first thing that made it stand out was where it took place, just behind the Royal Forest Hotel, near to Connaught Waters – yes, the same area where Mary Jane had taken the lives of her two children and had told that traveller that she wanted to be taken to the police. The next detail which piqued my interest was the fact that he was released in January 1928 to the care of his brother – it was a clear-cut murder case, and he wasn't sentenced to death or even life imprisonment? I knew from everything else I have delved into that this normally meant a plea of insanity (similar again to Mary Jane) and was interested to know more.

On the evening of the 19th October, 1920, a man (we now know to have been Bartlett) alerted someone cycling past the hotel that there was a dead woman just near the tree, and the poor person he had told rode off to alert the police, but when he came back, Bartlett had gone. The woman (Caroline Jervis, known as Bessie) was lying as if asleep, but on further examination by the police it was quite evident she had been strangled and some of her clothes had been removed. Shortly after this discovery, letters started arriving at the homes of Bessie's family members, and Bartletts stating that they were fed up and frustrated with his family trying to separate them and had decided that Bessie was to take poison and that Albert would drown himself in Connaught Waters. This was the story he stuck by during the process of being charged. He said that Bessie had taken Salts of Lemon (oxalic acid, a type of bleaching agent) and was so distraught by her violent symptoms that her sweetheart Albert finished her off by strangling her – this was also how he explained her missing some of her clothes, that she had stripped them off in her frenzy.

The pathologist on the case was the now-famous Sir Bernard Spilsbury and he identified that Bessie was in the very early stages of pregnancy and had also recently had sexual intercourse. Was this the trigger for Albert or was something else at play?

Amazingly for a police force in 1920, the investigation was incredibly thorough, although I have found errors in some of the witness reports which did make me think that Albert was not being totally honest with his family and may have been very troubled and living a fantasy. Local chemists were contacted to see if Bessie had purchased this acid, and none of them recognised her. Then a Lancastrian woman called Beatrice Shaw wrote to Albert's parents to tell them that they had a grandson, also called Albert, and that their son was refusing to take any responsibility for his child. Had this triggered his rage against his fiancée - the woman he was due to marry later that year? Had she told him she was pregnant, and he did not want to know?

It soon became evident that the killer had serious mental health problems, he was delusional about events, telling his family he had organised rooms for he and Bessie and talking about her as if she were still alive. This is where I think the story becomes even more sad and shows the effect that wartime had on the young men of the day. Albert had joined the Army on 3rd , 1913, as a member of the Border Regiment, and according to the military records, he went out to France on 25th November, 1914, so would have been one of the earlier divisions sent to that living hell. He was wounded at least twice by the June of 1915 – the records stating gunshot wounds – but he was sent back to Britain (a Blighty pass) on 22nd June 1916, with it stating "wounded and shell shock". One of the facts in the witness statements which shows me that he may have not been up front with his loved ones was that his father said to the police that he had been a Lance Corporal when he started the demobbing process and had been moved to the Royal Army Medical Corps in 1917.

This was not strictly true, and his conduct records show someone losing their ability to think rationally. On the 14th February, 1916, he was appointed a Lance Corporal but four months later, he was demoted back to Private under a charge of irregular conduct (using government property without permission), in fact, less than a year later he was in trouble again for interfering with the military police and using "filthy" language. The other error I found in what the family believed was that they were asked if there was any history of mental illness around them. Their answer was no, yet Albert's sister Lilian took her own life in 1909 aged just nineteen.

Albert had stayed in the Army after the end of the Great War, and was in Salonica (Greece) when it ended and also where he contracted malaria. From there he was in Russia during 1919 and then on to Germany as a member of the occupying forces. Another interesting fact was that he tended to disappear for two or three days at a time, every occasion returning to camp, being docked pay and going on as usual, all after his diagnosis of shell shock, which seems to be when his personality changed.

He also became a lot more sexually active, hospitalised with gonorrhoea in 1920, in early 1921 another sexually transmitted disease which he chose to keep quiet about until his commanding officer found out and yet again, docking of pay and stopping of leave. After he was taken to Broadmoor following his sentencing (and he is listed as being there in the 1921 census), his brother said that he would care for him and on 12th January 1928, he was released into his sibling's supervision. As before in the Army, he went walkabout, and at one point had three ladies come to the house looking for him. They said he owed them money and that he was supposed to have met them – the landlady of where these women were living kicked them out after just over a week as she did not approve of the type of lifestyle they led (it is quite obvious that they were sex workers, and that Albert was going to them for that very reason).

In September 1928, he was taken back to Broadmoor. We know that he was still there in 1939 but after that, we cannot say as the records are still closed. He was no angel; his education records say that he spent time in an industrial school (which were normally for children needing a strict hand) and at fourteen years old he was working as a French Polisher and then a casual labourer. It was not until after his shell shock diagnosis did he start exhibiting violent tendencies – he threatened Beatrice Shaw when she told him she was pregnant with his child, he also held a knife to Bessie's throat when he saw her talking to some other men at work and he said he wished he had killed his mother and sister as they were the ones that drove Bessie to "commit suicide". This is the reason I felt that this story fitted into this chapter, it made me wonder how many men had their brains altered inexorably due to war?

How many of these people committed crimes but their mental state was not taken into account? Albert had not had any disciplinary action documented against him until after that final injury, it is hard not to conclude that were it not for that, he would not have killed his fiancée and spent the rest of his days in Broadmoor.

Chapter 6 – Prisons and Prisoners

Every place has a dark past, regardless of how idyllic it may initially appear; the Essex forests are certainly no different as you have probably gathered even if you are reading chapters individually rather than concurrently. I thought I would focus this chapter on those areas which held people prisoner and the facilities that supported them.

As a district, the towns and conurbations which make up larger areas of the forest had not historically had a prison or bridewell for incarceration. Most court and arrest records show the majority being removed to Ilford or Chelmsford, but that is not to say that places did not spring up for this purpose – albeit not always the obvious.

The outbreak of the First World War gave the government cause to create internment camps, for both captured fighters of the other side, but also for those deemed to be a threat to British security. Many of these camps were in places like the Isle of Man, however there was a definite use for German soldiers who had the experience as many had come from an agricultural background in their home land as farm labourers.

These men could be kept in the prison hulks moored off the coast at Southend on Sea (short term whilst more substantial accommodation was being constructed, some were kept in the workhouses like Dunmow, Chelmsford and Rochford, and some if injured, would be kept in military hospitals/prisons like Colchester or Purfleet. Although, you may think they were the model of decorum but a quick look through the newspapers of the time does show quite a few complaints regarding those housed at Dunmow Workhouse, such as this in the Chelmsford Chronicle on 28th June 1918, after the regular Guardians meeting:

...the Master of the Workhouse, Mr. W. R. Errington, reported that considerable damage was being done by the German prisoners of war quartered at Workhouse. The prisoners jumped about the premises, played football on. Sundays, trampled down flower beds, scaled walls, climbed the roof of the Workhouse and crawled about like a lot of cats...

The Master also complained that they threw missiles at him after he took their football away, I doubt that kind of behaviour was not something he had to encounter on a regular basis running a workhouse, but the Guardians would have been paid to hold these prisoners. It also transpired that men from Dunmow who were being used for farm work were refusing to do anything, and the War Office was to be told, which is why the stories from the Chigwell area of Essex are interesting.

Whilst the rationing in W.W.1 was not as prevalent as W.W.2, the creation of food was still a necessary plan and the War Agricultural Executive Committee were tasked with increasing production in all the British counties. In Epping Forest and its surrounding grounds, an expanse in Hainault (near Chigwell Row) of around one-hundred -and-fifty acres was agreed to be handed over and ploughed, ready to be farmed by Foxburrow Farm nearby. Locals recounting their experiences of the Great War to historical webpages went over what happened at the site, explaining that over two-hundred German prisoners (which would have included navy, zeppelin crews and soldiers) would bunk down in three large barns at the farm and work the land, but do not worry that they were treated as slaves, they were paid for their toil.

There was certainly a lot of supervision for these men, in fact, in mid-April 1918 a baker from Ongar, William John Maryon was taken to court for selling fifteen loaves of bread to German P.O.W. who were based at Paslow Hall (High Ongar) and were working in Stondon Massey nearby. It was said that this kind of trade was a prelude to an escape attempt, and the authorities worked hard to prove whether Maryon was complicit or merely someone thinking he was doing the right thing by feeding prisoners of war – he was found to have been simply naïve and as he had an unblemished record, let off with a fine of a sovereign.

Another case, a few months later and a different part of Essex, took place in Leaden Roding, not a million miles away from the forest, where an eighteen-year-old bakers assistant by the name of Eva Charge was up in court charged with supplying six loaves of bread to German prisoners, and this was not her first time. These were men based at Dunmow workhouse (they already have a bit of a bad reputation in this chapter do they not?) and they were working the fields at Chalks Farm. Miss Charge was driving past and a few men leapt up and grabbed the reins of her horse, demanding bread. She told the authorities that she was terrified, and that these five men were unsupervised, there was no military presence around and she gave them the loaves for her own safety. Possibly to cover his own backside (my words, not the language used by the petty sessions as I am sure you can imagine) the adjutant to the camp, Lieutenant Collin Downey said that this kind of action could facilitate an escape - as with limited English, they would try and stockpile as much food as possible – and in the least, cause discipline issues in the camp.

That is not to say that the adjutant was wrong, there were certainly many escape attempts from these relatively lax prisons, and I shall mention a couple which I think show the strength of intent. Towards the end of August 1918, three German prisoners of war escaped from the Bishops Stortford centre which was looking after them. They managed to walk the nearly thirty miles to Maldon without being detected, and then stole a small boat with the plan to row it all the way home to Germany – it was the eagle eyes of a local fisherman in Mersea Island who spotted it moored on the banks and reported it as suspicious. I have to say, I am impressed at walking that far, and then even thinking you could row a boat across an expanse of open sea three times the width of the Channel.

An attempted sea escape which faired a little better – although still not successful – took place on 18th September 1918, when five prisoners got out of the camp at Chigwell Row. Three of them were apprehended after only ten days on the run, but two managed to get out to sea, piloting a small sailboat, and were spotted by an Ipswich based captain who sailed between England and France for trade on a regular basis. It was one of His Majesty's patrol boats who brought them in, and they docked at Brightlingsea, having got quite a few miles away from the coast of England before being stopped.

But enough of W.W.1 and prisoner of war camps…for now anyway. There was a much more recent facility for incarceration within the forest boundaries which was there until 1969. In 1947, the owner of Hill Hall, Lady Hay, sold off her property to the Home Office. It took them some time to decide what to do with it, but in 1952 it was reopened but it was not the kind of place that the general public would want to visit, as it was a low security women's prison. The facility was publicised as "an experimental prison without bars", and to add to the originality of the place, it also had a female governor, fifty-three-year-old Miss Dorothy J. Wilson, a former deputy from Manchester prison, amongst others.

I am sure that there are people who remember Hill Hall being a women's prison, but there are many (including my husband!) who will be quite shocked that this building, which is now a luxury residence for those who can afford apartments at top end prices, was once the home of female lawbreakers.

There are quite a few interesting stories relating to its time as a jail, but you can refer to my chapter on buildings of the forest for more information on this particular place. There is a very famous case where the lady "villain" of the piece was held here, but let us look at some less well known ones first, shall we?

A quick search of the newspapers at the time produced a story about the release after only four months of her six-month sentence of one Mrs. Mavis Wheeler. Whilst it is not the type of criminal case that may make a dramatic documentary on the crime channel, it is certainly an interesting one, and also a story that would most likely have caused a lot of gossip amongst the upper-class circles.

On the 30th July 1954, divorcee Mavis Wheeler shot married Lord Anthony Vivian with a revolver, and seriously wounded him in the stomach – all seems clear cut? Well not so much. It transpires that Wheeler and Vivian had been spending most of their time together since the previous summer and he had been – more or less – living in her London home, and spending alternate weekends at her cottage in Potterne, Wiltshire. What is interesting about the newspaper reports is that only one I found made any reference to wondering how his wife felt (they had been married since 1930) but nearly all passed judgement on how Wheeler was dressed when appearing in any formal setting.

"She did not deign to wear a hat" (oh the horror!)

"She wore peep toe shoes without tights" (the floozy!)

"She flaunted her blonde hair" (how dare she have blonde hair!)

Despite the incident happening in the July, it was not until October that it finally went to trial as rather than just the original charge of unlawful and malicious wounding, the prosecution wanted to increase the charge to attempted murder, although establishing a cause was proving quite tricky for them. Once Vivian was well enough to give evidence (albeit from his hospital bed) he told them how he and Mrs. Wheeler were absolutely devoted to each other and wished to marry, having already exchanged rings with that in mind.

He explained (and verified the evidence Mavis had given) that they had spent the evening at the local pub, and upon returning to Pilgrims Cottage, Mrs. Wheeler had been unable to locate the key, so he had jimmied a window open and climbed in. He had gone out again to get some beer from the pub, but had not told his partner this, and when he went to regain entry, he was shot. Most of his testimony mentions that he could not confirm beyond all doubt that it was Mrs. Wheeler, but that she did have an American Colt pistol, which was given to her at the end of the Second World War in 1945. Many of the newspaper reports also speak of his outpouring of love for his girlfriend, his longing to for them to be together all the time and it being her who told him to go home to his wife and son for Christmas.

His wife Victoria was there to hear all of this, if I was writing this as a novel, it would have been her hiding in the shadows of the cottage. It would have been her who shot her husband to have it look like his mistress did it and to get her out of the way easily…

To cut a long story short, Mavis was found guilty not of attempted murder, but the original charge of unlawful and malicious wounding and sentenced to six months in prison – of which she served only four months at Hill Hall Prison without bars in Theydon Mount. On the 2nd February 1955, she was driven out of Hill Hall via a little-used side exit to meet with Lord Vivian at Epping train station, where she was whisked away in a chauffeur driven limousine to her property in London and life with the devoted peer.

I did have a look to see if they did ever get officially married, and I could find no trace of it, with Anthony staying together with his wife, and passing away in 1991. Obviously, no-one really knows if Victoria was agreeable with anything that happened, whether they were just married in name only and if this was the first time that the man she had married in 1930 was inclined to marry himself (even if common law) to another woman, I can still imagine how scandalous it would have been in the 1950s.

Ironically – well, I think it is – as with all prisons, there were escapes and attempts to liberate themselves, but there were more escapes by male prisoners than female…from a women's prison. You have read that correctly, more male guests of her majesty's pleasure got away from Hill Hall than women. I am being slightly economical with the truth, but prisoners from places like Pentonville would be brought to work on the old Elizabethan Mansion, and some decided to make a bid for freedom whilst doing so.

That is not to say that some of the Hall's full-time guests did not try their luck too, on the 20th February, 1957, twenty-three-year-old Beatrice Mary Boyle stole over £217 worth of clothing and jewellery from Governor Wilson's home (where she had been employed as a maid) and ran.

In case you were wondering, the inflation tools on the internet estimate that amount to be around £5,000 in today's money.

Boyle's was an interesting story, she had been arrested in March 1956 for assaulting and robbing her landlady, Mrs. Winifred Bittleston. She had not acted alone however, and whilst she got a two year sentence her boyfriend, David Hills, was given four years. What made it something that the newspapers seemed to very much enjoy covering was that she had left her baby in the local Woolworths so that he was not involved in the crime – the baby was not Hills' child. Boyle was actually married (in 1954, she had become hitched to William Boyle, her maiden name was Mathias) and her son was born in 1955. During her court case, it became evident that her and Hills were broke and starving, and were hoping that by attacking Bittleston with a hammer, they would be able to get some money from her to buy food.

I do wonder what happened to Beatrice and her son, and hope that they managed to find their path when she was released.

The most famous prisoner held at Hill Hall was probably Christine Keeler, she of the Profumo scandal notoriety, but so much has been written about the incident that there is not much to add…however I do have another case that was to do with national security and involved a woman.

Barbara Fell was a high-ranking employee within the Central Office of Information (C.O.I.), with her role as acting controller of Overseas Division. The C.O.I. was the successor to the Second World War Ministry of Information and could be best described as the Government's marketing and communication department.

On the 7th December, 1962, she pleaded guilty to eight charges under the Official Secrets Act and was sentenced to two years in prison, but what had she done? The fifty-four-year-old (the age she was when convicted) woman had been in a romantic relationship with Yugoslavian embassy press officer, Smiljan Pecjak, and had passed him information and documents which he had not been authorised to see. In her opinion, even though he was a citizen of a country that was behind the iron curtain, he was very enamoured by the west and its ways, and wanted to bring the ideology home.

Was Fell being made an example of? Even the news reports of the time felt that the judge, when sentencing, had not taken fully into account the Crown's statement that they had accepted that Fell had not done any of this with an intention to the prejudice of state interest or safety. As with most cases, an appeal was due to be lodged but she was refused the right to do so, apparently because as a senior member of staff, she could have accessed much more secure and potentially damaging documents.

One must wonder if it was partly to do with her standing as a high-ranking professional woman and also the fact - heaven forbid – she had been in a relationship. Interestingly, it was even mentioned in parliament in January 1963 when Sir T. Moore asked the then Chancellor of the

Exchequer if they would consider offering her a new position due to her experience. He made a point of saying that he had not met her, but surely she had paid an incredibly high price for indiscretion, especially as she had not been found guilty of spying.

She spent some time at Hill Hall and was then moved to Askham in York - another open prison – to finish her sentence. It was a sort of happy ending for Barbara, as after her release in the May of 1964 she married her former work colleague John Langston, the C.O.I. Head of Radio.

The Tatler was its normal witty self when mentioning Hill Hall in an article published on the 13th August 1966 saying:

London is to lose one of its best-known nicks: the Home Office are planning to abandon Holloway Prison and move its inmates to an extension of Hill Hall open prison at Theydon Garnon, Essex. A large new building will go up next to the historic mansion itself. At the moment the site is ringed with large notices: "Trespassers Will Be Prosecuted." And if found guilty, allowed to stay?

Hill Hall's incarnation as a prison was not to last indefinitely, however. On 18th April, 1969, a fire which began in the clothing store and records office of the north wing took hold incredibly quickly, and despite the efforts of over one-hundred firemen to quell the blaze, the hall was destroyed – although there were no casualties and all fifty-three prisoners were led to safety, which is a semi miracle in itself. That was the end of the hall's use as a facility of imprisonment

The Elements of Epping Forest

(even without bars), and it was left fire damaged and quasi-derelict for many years.

In the interests of not wanting to upset people however, I would not suggest going to the grounds of Hill Hall to try and conduct an investigation or two, because these days it is very much *not* derelict and actually a very luxurious complex of apartments. Trespassing on the site would run you the risk of upsetting the boys 'n gals in blue (well, black and white these days), so I would not advise or suggest it. There are plenty more places in the area of what was the Forest of Essex that you can explore.

Whilst there were not a huge number of W.W.2 prisoner of war camps in the forest itself, there were those being sent from the surrounding centres (Hatfield Heath probably being the closest) to work on the farms and even in some places to help build new homes – Melbourne Estate in Chelmsford, I am looking at you here. That does not mean however that the area that includes Epping, Hainault and Waltham forests did not get a mention in a few articles of note.

One thing you notice when looking at the treatment of prisoners of war in the U.K. was that the death rate was not especially high, and whilst some did complain about food or lack of satisfactory work clothing, most got on with their lot and did what they were asked to – being able to leave the confines of your hut every day to labour in the open air must have been better than what their Allied equivalent were facing. I know for a fact that both Italian and German prisoners were made to feel very welcome by the British, would even attend the family mealtimes for Sunday dinner (that was told to me first-hand by an old Chelmsford farmer who was a teenager when his father had local prisoners of war helping with the agricultural side of things) and some went as far as marrying British girls.

That is my first story, and this is Werner Vetter of Chingford. Talk about biting the hand that fed you…

Vetter was a German Panzer trooper who had been captured and was being held in the U.K. as a prisoner of war, according to his words when in court, he explained how he had been forced to abandon his studies at a seventeen-year-old boy and go to fight for a mad leader in a war in which he wanted no part. He was a trailblazer of sorts however, as in May 1946, he met nineteen-year-old Olive Reynolds and they fell for each other hard, in fact, she admitted that she had gone into the woods with him at 10pm, not reappearing until 4am in the morning. Perhaps inevitably, as they were spending that much time together, she got pregnant and gave birth to a daughter. In that time though it was illegal for German prisoners of war to fraternise romantically, let alone marry a British girl and he was taken to court when their little girl was around ten weeks old. He received a twelve-month prison sentence without hard labour, and perhaps some may have thought that was the end of the relationship, but it was not. Between the two of them, they gave such an impassioned plea to the powers that be to change the rules surrounding this, and on 28th September, 1947 they were married at a church in Hampton Lovett in Worcestershire. Their honeymoon was mere hours together as Vetter had to return to his camp by 10pm, but eventually he was released and they set up home together in Chingford, whilst also battling for this former German prisoner of war to be granted citizenship.

An amusing sidenote to this story before I conclude it: Olive's widowed mother Beatrice was struggling financially after the wedding because her daughter chose to leave the home they shared in Chingford and move to a room closer to her new husband. If that was not harsh enough, her seventeen-year-old sister was getting engaged to a German sailor who was based in Worcestershire and had also left the area. In March 1948, the publicity surrounding this had reached a single farm worker near King's Lynn who offered marriage to fifty-year-old Beatrice, and she accepted.

Despite Olive and her husband only having spent mere weeks together, she was pregnant with their second child and in early June 1948 found out that her spouse was not being granted citizenship and was being repatriated back to Russian-held Germany – not something anyone would have wanted, even more so with hindsight! They battled with the Home Office, and finally towards the end of the same month that he was due to be deported, he was given permission to remain.

I made a "joke" about biting the hand and all of that - in January 1949, Werner was in court for house breaking, and as the police dug deeper, they found more cases against him including fencing stolen goods. Now, there was no choice, and he was expelled from England and returned to Germany. In interviews Olive said she was planning to follow him, but all I can find is Verner travelling to New York from Hamburg in April 1956. One has to hope that his wife and children were able to join him and that it was not just a relationship of convenience to give him a reason to be free.

The camp that Vetter had spent a short time at was Lippitt's Hill in High Beech – now a police helicopter base and training area – originally the site of some very powerful anti-aircraft batteries to protect nearby London, but from the summer of 1944, a P.O.W. camp. There were a few memorable names associated with the place. As you enter there is a statue, carved by Rudi Webber, prisoner number 540177 and also it was the wartime residence of Walter Weiland, who liked the area so much that he stayed and ended up serving as the Mayor of Waltham Abbey for some time.

More about Lippitt's Hill in another chapter...

In a public announcement like the one I made about Hill Hall, I would not try and venture onto the site where the P.O.W. camp at Lippitt's Hill was, whilst the temptation may be high and it is a stone's throw from the wooded areas of the forest, you would most likely be met by someone very unhappy in uniform and asked politely to leave. You may however be able to visit the pub, The Owl, which has been the home of a public house since the eighteenth century (this is a recent re-development), have a nice cold pint and see what you can pick up right on the doorstep, "spirits" willing.

I mentioned earlier that the death rates in the Allied P.O.W. camps were not high at all, and for those who were based in or around Epping Forest, St. Margaret's Hospital (yes, the former workhouse) would have been the place they were treated if taken poorly. I found one sad death, although I cannot find the cause, of Georg Schneider (the newspaper who reported, who I shall leave nameless, did not even spell his name correctly) passed away at the age of thirty-three. Originally he was buried in Epping, but like so many prisoners of war, he was moved to the German cemetery at Cannock Chase, where he is in Plot 1, Row 10, Grave 395.

Chapter 7 – Kings and Queens

You may wonder why there is a separate chapter dedicated to the royal side of the forest, when the whole point of it in the first place was that it was owned by the Monarchy and it was they who ultimately controlled what happened there.

I have already touched upon the connection of King Harold Godwinson to the area, he was the person who built up the abbey at Waltham, and is also connected (or so the chroniclers say) to why it was known as "Waltham Holy Cross". The legend was first documented by a Canon of Waltham Abbey in the early twelfth century, and entitled "Liber de invention sanctae Crucis". It tells of a common labourer who had a dream (during the reign of King Canute) of where to find a cross, which would be the very "sign of Christ's passion". After receiving the same vision three times, the man was imbued with a sense of purpose and went to the area in Montacute, Somerset and there found a life-size crucifix (sometimes called a Holy Rood). When the owner of the estate, Tovi, had this find communicated to him, he commanded that the relic be transported to Canterbury, but the twelve oxen who were to pull this precious load would not move. He then suggested his house at Reading, still the beasts refused to budge, and it was only when he suggested his simple house in Waltham that the cattle began their journey. Whether this story is apocryphal or has any semblance of truth in it is unknown, but Harold placed much credence to the supernatural belief that this curio was related to Christ and it is even said to have cured him of paralysis.

Is Harold laid to rest at his beloved Waltham Church? Nobody knows for sure, but there are many who believe that after his death at Hastings, he was buried where he fell. We do not have many accounts from that time period to relate to, but thirteenth century chronicler, Robert of Gloucester wrote that "Wyllam yt send hyr vayre ynon wythoete enyhynge warnore, so that yt was born hyre with gret honour y bore, to the hous of Waltham, and ybrogt anerthe there, In the holy rode Chyrche, that he let him sulf rere". Before you ask, yes, I did go through in its entirety. For something originally written in the Middle Ages, it does actually make some sense if you speak it as opposed to just reading it, which is probably why, when trawling through the thousands of pages of the original works I was asked quite frequently by my children why I was talking to myself...not that it is unusual for me to have my own conversation.

In a nutshell, Robert of Gloucester seems to believe that William the Conqueror allowed Harold Godwinson's body to be taken back to Waltham Holy Cross and interred there, and although this particular historian is said to have been born around two hundred years after the events of Hastings, he is one heavily referred to for events of Britain up until around the end of the century in which he lived.

There is a story in a wonderful book called "Essex in the Days of Old", by Joseph Spurgeon about Henry VIII, we know that he was responsible for places like Waltham Abbey being stripped but he was apparently seen there quite frequently. On one occasion, he had been hunting in Epping Forest and had come to the abbey alone, in disguise, as one of his "common" guards. As dinner was just about to be served, he was invited to sit at the abbot's table. We know that Henry's appetite was legendary, but after a day of hunting he was particularly ravenous it seems, and the abbot, unaware of who exactly he was addressing said "I would willingly give a hundred pounds on condition I could feed as heartily on beef as thou dost."

Oops.

A few days later, the said abbot was summoned to London and immediately committed to the Tower – being fed on bread and water, he was unsurprisingly, confused as to what crime he was guilty of. A few days later, a choice cut of beef was set before him, and he attacked it with gusto, his meagre rations up until that point having rendered him rather hungry. As the meal was finished, the King suddenly entered, demanding the hundred pounds that the abbot had so recklessly promised for a heartier appetite. No heads rolled as a result of this, the money (the equivalent of around £40,000 now!) was paid, and the abbot went back to Waltham.

I have mentioned in another chapter about Elizabeth the First's love of hunting and the forest, but she would also visit the area before she became Queen. Her sister Mary had fled to Norfolk when she felt she was under threat from the reign of her younger brother (Edward VI 1547-1553). After his death, and when she started to realise that the support for the unfortunate Lady

Jane Grey becoming Queen was on the wane, she based herself at nearby Wanstead House (which was in the forest of Waltham) and her younger sister Elizabeth made the journey to see her, ostensibly to assure her of loyalty and support. Interestingly, this was not to be Elizabeth's only visit to Wanstead house. The infamous Robert Dudley, Earl of Leicester (he of Kenilworth Castle fame, and was he or was he not the Queens lover?) ended up owning it and we know that Elizabeth stayed there for five days in 1578.

Whilst future monarchs were not so keen to visit the forest for the same means of recreation regarding hunting after James I - the sojourns were more to the various big houses of the forest - it was still very much in use and that in part was down to Henry VIII. He had created the Navy, and they needed ships, and to build these vessels, vast quantities of wood needed to be sent to the various shipbuilding yards around the country (Chatham and Portsmouth in the main).

This was a copy of a letter sent regarding raw materials being taken from the Forest of Waltham, 5th May 1662, so during the reign of Charles II (1660 – 1685).

Photo author's own

Digressing slightly, when I was going through the admiralty papers that contained this letter (six boxes worth, this was the only mention I found of Waltham, and it only covered about three years!) I did find letters to and from one Samuel Pepys. When you realise you are touching documents that were handled by famous people in history such as him, it does send a weird tingle down your spine.

One of the biggest changes to occur came under Queen Victoria's reign; a variety of events had happened, but the one that appeared to ignite huge change was that of lopping. You may not be familiar with the practice, but the people of Loughton had an annual tradition (descending back to the time of Elizabeth I it is believed), where between the dates of 11th November and 23rd April each year, they could go into the forest and cut down branches of trees rising more than seven foot from the ground (the lower branches were food for deer and the suchlike). This fuel was used in lieu of coal and was also a way of maintaining the forest and I suppose, an early form of tree surgery. The issue was that those who felt they owned the land, such as John Whitaker Maitland, Rector of Loughton and the Lord of the Manor, wanted to exclude the people from accessing common ground which he felt was on his estate, not just for the practice of lopping, but also from grazing cattle. Throughout the larger area, wealthy Lords were selling what was ostensibly common land for development, and whilst Maitland offered a small amount of compensation, it was nowhere near comparable to what the locals lost. Local man Thomas Willingale was not happy about this and continued to practice this centuries-old tradition.

Ultimately however, when the Epping Forest Act of 1878 was heard, not only was enclosure of lands to be stopped (as the forest was to be declared totally public and to be managed by the City of London Corporation) but so was the practice of lopping. In fact, if you visit Loughton you can see a place called Lopping Hall, and this was built with the funds given to the parishioners for the loss of these rights. It was actually covered in detail during the debates, Sir John George Shaw Lefevre, who was actually a Barrister as well as a politician said (in relation to the Loughton inhabitants saying it was granted by the Tudor Queen):

There was no direct evidence of such a grant; but custom, from time immemorial, could be proved, and lawyers of eminence said that was sufficient. As to compensation, he did not think it would be right to compensate for the rights thus taken possession of by money; and he thought the best course to pursue would be for the Bill to acknowledge the right and leave it to an arbitrator to say what compensation should be given. If that were not done, great dissatisfaction would be created and great hardships would exist.

You can see from the page I have enclosed of the Act, that this was not the first one to be passed in Parliament, but it is to what most people refer when they talk about the gift of Epping forest to the people and away from royal (and landed gentry) rule and ownership.

It is said that the Queen understood the importance of this area of land to her people, especially those merely a stone's throw away in the East end who valued the opportunity to see green and taste clean natural air when they were able. As with all things Government related, the House of Commons accounts make for typical table tennis type reading, with objections and statements being batted backwards and forwards across the proverbial net, but Statesman William Cowper -Temple made a valid point:

He was glad the requirements of so large a body of the people were thus to be considered, and that they would have much-needed facilities for obtaining recreation and fresh air, and the other advantages to be derived from open spaces in a great Metropolis like this.

.

[41 & 42 Vict.]   *Epping Forest Act*, 1878.   [Ch. ccxiii.]

CHAPTER ccxiii.

An Act for the Disafforestation of Epping Forest and the pre- A.D. 1878.
servation and management of the uninclosed parts thereof
as an Open Space for the recreation and enjoyment of the
public; and for other purposes.   [8th August 1878.]

WHEREAS Epping Forest is part of the ancient Royal Forest Epping
of Waltham: Forest.

And whereas in February one thousand eight hundred and seventy 1870.
the Commons House of Parliament presented an address to Her Address of
Majesty the Queen, praying that she would take such measures Commons.
as in her judgment she might deem most expedient in order
that Epping Forest might be preserved as an open space for the
recreation and enjoyment of the public:

And whereas in answer thereto Her Majesty was graciously Answer of
pleased to express her concurrence in the desire that open spaces the Queen.
in the neighbourhood of the Metropolis might as far as possible be
preserved for the enjoyment of her people, and to promise that she
would carefully consider how effect might be given to the prayer of
the said address:

And whereas, in consequence of the said address, the Epping 1871-6.
Forest Act, 1871, was passed; which Act, after reciting the said Epping
address and answer, constituted a body of Commissioners, called the 34 & 35 Vict.
Epping Forest Commissioners, and enacted (among other things) to c. 93.
this effect: 35 & 36 Vict.
c. 95.

(1.) That the Commissioners should prosecute in relation to 36 & 37 Vict.
the Forest inquiries respecting the boundaries, rights, encroach- 38 & 39 Vict.
ments, and inclosures of, over, and in the Forest; c. 6.

(2.) That they should settle a Scheme for disafforesting the 39 & 40 Vict.
Forest and the preservation and management of its waste lands; c. 3.

(3.) That they should have the same powers as if those waste
lands were a common within the Metropolitan Commons Act, 1866, 29 & 30 Vict.
and they were the Inclosure Commissioners; c. 122.

(4.) That they might report any special arrangements with landowners or others in furtherance of the objects of the Scheme;

[Local.–213.]   A   1

It took a few years after the 1878 Act for everything to start changing hands (as with all Acts of Parliament, they never seem to be immediate unless it is for tax purposes!) and on 6th May 1882, Queen Victoria was scheduled to appear in the forest to make the handover to the public, and the disafforestation official – in case you are wondering, deforestation and disafforestation are two completely different things, the former means in effect, cutting down of trees to a huge extent, whereas the latter is a change in the legal ownership status, invariably from Royal ownership to common.

On that date, the crowds gathered to watch the Queen officially pass the forest to the people, and to relinquish over eight-hundred years of royal ownership and control. It must have been a genuinely majestic sight to see, the newspapers estimated over half a million people made the various journeys to watch Victoria's cortege pass through the High Beech area of the woods, and some of the parking rules as to where carriages could be left were removed whilst the celebrations were going on.

We are requested to state that on the occasion of the Queen visiting Epping Forest to-morrow, wheeled vehicles will be allowed to stand on the Forest along the Queen's route, provided that a clear space of not less than 30 feet in width, on either side of the road, be left for spectators on foot, and that the positions be occupied by the vehicles before two o'clock p.m London Evening Standard - Friday 05 May 1882

The Queen was due to arrive at Chingford at exactly five minutes past four.

She was accompanied by many dignitaries, including the mounted police, members of the forest sub reception committee, some of the verderers and also soldiers from the 1st Battalion Warwickshire and Essex Artillery Volunteers who were based at nearby Chingford.

With her, she had members of her immediate family, her daughters Louise and Beatrice, plus the Duchess of Connaught who was married to Prince Arthur, the Queen's seventh child who happened to be the newly appointed Ranger of the forest.

The presentation in front of the Kings Oak Hotel in the heart of the beautiful woodland was viewed by those with enough social reputation from within a large grandstand which seated around two-thousand – it also meant that Victoria could stay seated within her carriage. Whilst she was still to reign for another nineteen years after this, it was said she was getting quite reclusive and would rather not have to walk around if possible. As she was brought through a giant arch upon which the words read "God Save the Queen", she received the address from the Corporation of London. She said:

"I thank you sincerely for your loyal and dutiful address, and it gives the greatest satisfaction to dedicate this beautiful forest for the enjoyment of my people. I thank you for your continued solicitude for my welfare."

So, if you ever visit the Kings Oak Hotel, stand there, admire the beautiful oak tree (planted for Victoria herself), and just take yourself back to when the Forest of Waltham became public domain.

Chapter 8 - Institutions

You did not think I would talk about an area as huge as Epping Forest and not be able to factor in some information regarding asylums and workhouses surely?

One of the names which kept coming up in my research was that of Dr. Matthew Allen, and his involvement with Fairmead House. The treatment of those with mental health issues was still developing, and it was almost accepted that it was just a way of keeping those people off the streets and away from the possibility of being an embarrassment to their families. By the time Allen was born in 1786, things had started to change, albeit incredibly slowly. In 1774, five men appointed by the Royal College of Physicians, took on the role of commissioners in lunacy to both inspect and regulate asylums within a seven-mile radius of London, however this was not enough to stop cruelty and maltreatment in other parts of the country. An article published in volume 384 of the Lancet on 19th July, 2014 entitled "A tale of whistleblowing and lunacy laws" talks about a batch of communications written to the secretary of state, Robert Peel, by former stockbroker Trophimus Fulljames. He himself had been sent to the incredibly expensive private Brislington House Asylum in Bristol, run by Quaker Edward Long Fox and modelled on the moral treatment ideas of York Retreat – a revolutionary establishment opened in 1796 which forbade manacling patients or physically punishing them. It could be said that Fox was perhaps disingenuous in his adverts of Brislington being based on the ethical and revolutionary approach of York as Fulljames certainly painted a bleak picture. He spoke of residents who were totally sane and had been placed there by relatives, and worse, some of the punishments that were meted out to those shut up inside. A favourite method of treatment was the cold shower with the emphasis on the shock part of it, locking patients up in dark stone cells with no human interaction, and the one that for anyone claustrophobic would induce panic - shutting them in coffins. The investigators found no medical purpose for this; it was purely for the amusement of sadistic keepers.

Unfortunately however, there was no understanding of fluctuating lucidity as we would identify now, and Fulljames was found to be delusional, and his writings - albeit complex and full of viable facts – were discounted. It did not help when Peel had written to Dr. Fox at Brislington and accepted his version of events unequivocally (plus the signatures of former keepers confirming it all as rubbish). There were other events at play however, and it did cause committees to be formed between 1807 and 1827 to investigate the treatment of "lunatics" and to ensure those who were sane were not institutionalised unnecessarily and to guarantee good treatment for the genuinely ill.

Introducing Dr. Matthew Allen...he had worked at the hospital in York for five years and believed very strongly that you could cure people of these conditions with kindness and understanding as opposed to violence and bullying. This insight led him to form Fairmead or as it is on the 1841 Census records "Dr. Allen's private lunatic asylum" in the High Beech area of Epping Forest. Allen opened his facility in the Lippitts Hill area back in 1825 (two years before he married Elizabeth Blane Patterson, more of her later) and decided to take three houses and form them into a residence which would cater for those with mental health problems. Of the different buildings, Springfield would cater towards women, Leopards Hill Lodge (or sometimes known as Lippitts Hill Lodge) would be for men only and Fairmead would be occupied by Allen himself and have a mixture of both men and women living there. I mentioned earlier the changes to mental health supervision above, and from 1828, proprietors of private asylums had to apply for a yearly renewable license to run. It is fascinating to read the records in the Essex archives which show the information that Allen gave to the relevant quarter sessions as and when he was required.

For example, we know that in 1835, he applied for the permissions in respect of the three buildings confirming that Fairmead would have a mixture of fifteen "male/female/insane" and then with a comment marked with a star saying "not paupers". Springfield house was to have fifteen women and be run by Mrs. Esther Hall, and Leopards thirty insane men and run by a widowed farmer by the name of Mr. William Hockdale. Allen went into detail in the submission advising that it would be those of a "decided" nature who would be housed at Leopard, but it is the further information that shows why historians today joke about the place being 'The Priory' of the 19th century. All residents were able to have their own separate quarters if they so wished, this would affect the maximum number which he was able to care for in each, but not just that, there was room accounted for, should they have attendants who would be living there with them – in the Fairmead designs, a large room in the attic was designated as the servant's bedroom. The ethos of care that Allen and his team provided had an emphasis on kindness, at Fairmead for example the genders were encourage to mix together as he believed it was a good way of regulating mood and temperament by the sexes learning from each other.

Whilst these buildings were designed to look like a large family home, the internal layout was designed with the illness that was being treated in mind, with areas for noisier patients set aside slightly from the main traffic of people. Various places for those living there to sleep included dormitory style but also individual bedrooms. There was one architectural feature that made me chuckle when I was looking at the nearly two-hundred-year-old drawings, Springfield (the one for women) had a beer store…now I know that weak beer was drunk frequently as it was healthier than water, but it still amused me slightly. This may sound flippant, and it certainly is not meant to cast any doubt on the genuine treatment that Allen was looking to offer people but I know my husband would love it if I asked an architect to draw a specific room into our home to store beer!

In his essay on the classification of the insane, published in 1837, Allen specified that these homes were to consist of:

A front or what may be called the family portion of the house with galleries behind, with appropriate rooms for patients requiring more restraint.

The different areas would mean that those being treated could move from the more intensive side to the family orientated side, meaning any painful associations with their illness would not be a constant reminder and potential for relapse. Although when you dig deeper into the past of Dr. Allen, some quite disturbing stories do come to light which explain why the asylum was perhaps doomed to ultimate financial failure. He was an unreliable child, with a circle of what his family felt were unsuitable friends. Marrying at nineteen years old, his wife died around four years later and he left York and ended up finding wife number two. Setting up a business in Edinburgh, his older brother Oswald found out where Matthew was when he received a bill for unpaid rent on the shop that his sibling was running. Allen spent time in debtors prison over the next ten years, and somehow received a medical degree in 1821 but left York asylum in 1824. Whilst Allen said it was with full commendations from the Governors, his brother said he was fired due to improper behaviour towards the physician.

Whatever the truth was, Allen had started off his medical career as an apothecary, but even still, his views on the treatment of mental health were well received.

He treated the poet John Clare at Fairmead. The writer had many strange delusions, thinking he had two wives, Patty and Mary (he did not), believed himself to be a prize fighter and at times, imagining himself as Lord Byron. Dr. Allen wrote to a large newspaper saying:

It is most singular that ever since he came...the moment he gets pen or pencil in hand he begins to write most poetical effusions. Yet he has never been able to obtain in conversation, nor even in writing prose, the appearance of sanity for two minutes or two lines together, and yet there is no indication of insanity in any of his poetry.

Clare managed to give the attendants at Fairmead the slip (there was a policy of allowing some patients to walk freely, and it was a voluntary stay as opposed to mandated in most cases), when he walked the eighty miles home, turning up at the house of his first love Mary (to whom he believed he was married), refusing to believe her family that she had perished in a house fire some years previously.

Another famous name associated with Allen was Alfred Tennyson, the poet. His family had been residing at a house nearby in High Beech and he developed a close friendship with the Doctor. The physician always had his next-get-rich-quick scheme in mind, and an automated wood carving machine called the pyroglyph was one he managed to convince Tennyson to invest his family fortune in, subsequently losing all the money and sending the poet into a deep depression. It is somewhat ironic that a man who professed to want to cure people of mental illness, drove someone else into the depths of an episode due to his recklessness with money and finance.

Allen passed away in January 1845, and his wife tried to continue running the hospital as best as she could. The 1851 census shows Elizabeth as the proprietor of Fairmead House Asylum, with seven patients and eight servants living there. In 1853 there was an administrative summons in respect of the late Dr. Allen, made by Walker Skirrow of Heaton, Mersey, with Elizabeth Allen defending. The quarter sessions show that the hospital was still operating in 1855 but what happened between then and the 1861 census, when Springfield was lived in by agricultural workers? One can only guess that it had become financially unviable and had to be shut down. The buildings were demolished in the 1870s, so many people are totally unaware of the history of mental health medicine that was created in that small part of Epping Forest.

Another institution that was in the heart of the woodland was the Epping Poor Law Union (P.L.U.) workhouse (you did not think you would get a book out of me that avoided talking about workhouses, did you? You should know by now that they get mentioned whenever I have the opportunity.)

After the Poor Law Amendment Act of 1834, unions were created after an amalgamation of various parishes, some (like in the inner-city areas of London and Manchester) would only have a couple within their remit, others like Epping, consisted of eighteen different territories including Chigwell, Chingford, Harlow, Loughton and

Theydon Bois. The other large area of the forest, Waltham Abbey, was part of the Edmonton P.L.U.

On the 16th January 1836, the Epping P.L.U. was formed and building began on the workhouse to be situated in the area now known as the Plain (although back then, it was the Chelmsford Turnpike). By early 1838 it was ready to accept admissions and was expected to accommodate around two- hundred to two-hundred-and-twenty inmates (inmate being the term used as opposed to resident).

There was an account I found from Epping Poor Law Union's early days that had me shaking my head. I appreciate that for the overseer and Poor Law Union board, they were operating under a different principal to how they did before, but common sense did seem to be lacking in this example. Benjamin Ellis was not a workshy man, he was working as a labourer and providing for his wife and eight young children but on Friday 26th October 1838, he applied to the Governors for some out relief to help him buy flour – he explained that after his rent was paid, he had about eight shillings left with which to feed and clothe his large family. The Board refused, and said his only option was to go into Epping Workhouse, which would cost around £1 and five shillings a week...go figure the logic on that one! He was sent to Ilford Gaol for fourteen days for refusing to work in the gardens of the house, even though he explained to the Magistrate that it was not due to him not wanting to work, it was that his shoes were not suitable.

In case you are wondering what happened to Benjamin, his wife Eliza and their family? They left the workhouse and moved to Waltham Holy Cross.

The first census taken in 1841 shows just over one-hundred-and-forty-people linked to the workhouse in Epping, although some of those could have been staff working there, such as the Master and the Matron.

In 1846, tenders from building firms were invited for the construction of the Infirmary, which foreshadowed the eventual use of the site as with so many workhouses of the nineteenth century.

A lot of the reports I can find were to do with the then Master, Edmund Champness. If you look through the newspaper reports of the time, he is mentioned quite frequently as there definitely appeared to be a slightly unruly element residing at the Workhouse. In 1844, five male inmates were charged with unruly behaviour. Their crime? They had scaled the wall into the women's yard and were caught trying to enter the women's rooms through an open window – men and women were kept separate, for obvious reasons!

In March 1848, two labourers, twenty-one-year-old George Wilson, and seventeen-year-old John Smith were brought up in front of the courts on a charge of arson. In August of the previous year, the cry of fire had been sounded. Champness went to investigate and found both the men's and women's wing of the casual's unit (tramps in other words) aflame, whilst trying to rescue those inside he found one of the male casuals, O'Brien, badly burned. Their excuse to the courts for the fire was that they had lit a match to look for a farthing that had been dropped – the mattresses they slept on were stuffed with straw, I will leave you to draw your own conclusions on whether that would have been a sensible thing to do or not – but a neighbour who had come forward to try and help put out the flames saw Wilson leaning nonchalantly against a wall, telling anyone who would listen that he "intended to burn the whole bloody place down". It did not go too well for both these young men, and they were sentenced to transportation for fifteen years.

In January 1850, Edmund's name appears again, charging Caroline Archer, Charlotte Stacey, Elizabeth Springham and Sarah Banks with disorderly conduct in the house, they all received three weeks hard labour at Ilford Gaol.

If any of you are wondering where on earth Ilford Gaol was, it shut in 1878 and is now the site of a petrol station and loads of houses.

There are sometimes stories of inmates in the Workhouse finding love, but Edmund was to find his wife whilst working as the Master as she was the Matron, a widow named Alice Guppy Jeffery. Even though she was eighteen years his junior, they married in late 1850, and in August 1860 when Champness passed away (at that point, working as a tea dealer in East London), Alice was mentioned in his Will.

Around thirty years after the original infirmary was built, the history books talk about it being extended and modernised, this is something you see quite frequently when looking at the history of many of the Poor Law workhouses, but why? Prior to the 1870's, the standard of medical care in workhouses left a lot to be desired. The infirmaries were normally too small, had to mix different patients (sometimes even sharing a bed), there were no trained nurses with female inmates doing the role and the Medical Officer was a position given to invariably the cheapest medical practitioner they could find. These Doctors would either be incredibly inexperienced, incompetent and unable to earn through private practice or even doing it as a part time job alongside their fee-earning work.

It was the Medical Officer for the Strand workhouse, Joseph Rogers M.D. who published an incredibly critical piece in The Lancet in 1865, who began to change the approach to healthcare in the house. Coupled with the nursing advances being pioneered by the legendary Florence Nightingale, things began to change. I could probably do a whole chapter on workhouses and their care of the sick, but as this is about Epping Forest and its associate towns and villages, I will save that for another day. Hopefully this quick explanation is sufficient to outline the main reason why you see so many workhouses increasing their infirmary size and changing how they were managed.

This is a sad story that I read in the Essex Newsman, 5th March 1881:

Inquest.—An inquest was held on Thursday at the Epping Union Workhouse on the body of a woman known as the "Tip toe" Gipsy. It appeared that she was found by her brother and sister in her tent in Hainult Forest insensible. They placed her in a donkey cart and got order from the relieving officer to remove her to the workhouse, took them about six hours, to reach the house, and when examined by the medical officer the deceased was pronounced to be dead. On a post-mortem examination being made it was ascertained that she had died from coagulation of blood in the right ventricle of the heart. The jury found a verdict accordingly.

It does make you start to question that if they had been able to go directly to the infirmary, could she have survived? Also, just how many people were living in the various smaller parts of the forest, even in the latter part of the 19th century?

It was not just older people who would pass away at the workhouse. Because so many were taken there for medical help, a younger person was just as likely to take their last breath as someone of more senior years. Take this story from the Essex Herald 8th September 1884:

An inquest was held by Mr. W. B. Blood (deputy coroner) the Epping Workhouse on Saturday morning on the body of a man supposed to be Harry Newlan, a horse coper, 25 years of age, of Wyndham-road, Camberwell, who died at the Workhouse on the previous day under distressing circumstances.—Deceased, it appeared, had been getting his living in a precarious manner in the Forest during the summer, and about six o'clock on Monday evening, the 1st inst., be was outside the Prince of Wales public-house, Chingford Hatch, when a man gave him a penny with which to obtain half pint of beer. He procured the beer, was seen drinking it, smoking cigarette, and reading newspaper. Nothing further was seen of him, however, until ten o'clock on the following when he was found lying in an insensible condition in the stable of the Prince of Wales Inn man named Geo. Faint. Information was given to the Woodford, and Inspector Hunnisett immediately summoned Dr. Roberts (the police divisional surgeon), who attended and advised the poor fellow's removal to the Epping Workhouse, which was done. He never regained consciousness, however, and died half-past three o'clock on Friday morning.— Dr. Galloway said he had no doubt death resulted from effusion of blood on the brain.— The jury returned verdict Death from natural causes."

For those wondering just what a horse coper is, it means a dealer and in fact, one description of that particular role mentioned how they were always smarmy and dishonest! An effusion of blood translates really to a head injury, so I wonder how they came to the conclusion it was natural causes?

You can see from these articles how the workhouse was also the go-to place for any kind of medical emergency, it was not just an establishment for able-bodied poor who were out of work and could not find a salary, many of the inmates were actually classed as non-able bodied (in the terminology, infirm or aged) and due to the cost of an individual needing to go into a Poor Law Asylum as opposed to a workhouse was around eight or nine times as much, so if the P.L.U. could get away with them going to the latter to be cared for, they would.

An example came in July 1895 that backfired badly when a male pauper who had been moved from The Strand P.L.U. to Epping lost his hold on reality and severely attacked two other inmates. Early reports said he had nearly killed them, which was confirmed to be an exaggeration, but his mental condition was serious enough that he was moved very quickly to the Asylum at Brentwood.

The next big change for Epping P.L.U. came during the First World War when the Army requisitioned the area as they were expecting huge numbers of casualties coming in from the East End docks.

In 1930, control of the workhouse was passed from the board of Governors to local authority control, and it became a Public Assistance Institution. Eight years later, the infirmary was renamed St. Margaret's Hospital which it is still known as now (although nearly all traces of its past use have been erased).

The Second World War saw it pulled into military use again, as were so many medical facilities, and whilst you may recollect the bombing of the maternity home that I mentioned in another chapter that occurred in 1940, the hospital was also the site of many deaths. On the 22nd March 1945, according to the records, at 2.44am, a V2 rocket hit the water tower on Fairfield street. The resulting explosion and cascade of water flooded both nearby houses and parts of St. Margarets, including the elderly unit of the hospital and the casuals wing of the workhouse. It resulted in the deaths of seven men, the oldest at eighty-two, and the youngest at thirty.

There are other institutions that were based in Epping Forest and its surrounding area, such as Chigwell school which was founded in 1629 by

The Archbishop of York and Vice Chancellor of Cambridge University, Samuel Harsnett.

It has an interesting history itself, but one of the most well-known of its alumni is probably William Penn, the very same Penn which Pennsylvania is named after...although those of us who watch breakfast tv and "Tipping Point" are probably more likely to say "oh, I know that name!" when presenter Ben Shephard is mentioned.

Back to poor unions - the powers that be realised that having children in the workhouse may not have been the best upbringing for them, and whilst many of the other inmates were there for reasons such as pure poverty, some may have had a less than beneficial influence on impressionable young minds. From the mid - 19th century, they started to create what were known as cottage homes for these children, run by "foster" parents who tried to replicate a caring, secure environment. Originally, in the earlier part of their development, they were for the more wayward and delinquent youngsters, and proved quite successful in correcting the potentially dangerous path they were treading. In doing so, soon it was realised that it was actually worthwhile for all children to be able to attend if possible.

Epping was a little bit slow to this particular party it has to be said, and although they secured the land from the farmer who owned it in 1902, and also secured a loan for £1,807 in 1903, the home itself was not opened until 1912 under its first matron, Alice Fleming – who even after her retirement from the role appears to have stayed in the area – just up from the St. Albans church in Coopersale Common in the heart of the forest and a few miles from Epping. From 1930 it came under the governance of the local authority as a public assistance institute (and if you want to look at the 1939 register for details, type in Cottages Homespublic (sic) Assistance Institution…you are welcome). In 1939, the lead foster mother was Hilda Oakley and it looks like they had at least forty children living with them, as was the number it had been originally designed for, and there are even stories of them visiting a swimming pool in the forest itself.

The home eventually closed in 1960 and was demolished shortly after. The area is now full of modern-day properties but if you are interested in sight-seeing, and wondered about the location, numbers 84-102 of Coopersale Common Road would be a good starting point.

Do you want to finish with an intriguing story about a possible resident of either St. Margarets, or the cottage home? No-one is quite sure which…Alan Francis Withers was born in 1933 to Francis and Hilda and was in 1939, living in Waltham Abbey with his parents. He became very ill with various ailments, including Tuberculosis, for which his family it seems gave him away to the authorities. He ended up less than five feet tall, with a severe spinal deformity and a long list of other disabilities. It was after he started donning a Stetson and singing Country and Western songs around the bars of London that he was to find his passion in life and re-named himself "Tex" Withers. By all accounts he was an amiable chap although he did try and persuade anyone who would listen that he was born in the United States and not North London, as was on his birth certificate.

Tex married his Native American "squaw" (as he called her) Light Fawn, and would even turn up to gigs on horseback! Sadly, he never hit the bigtime and died in 1987 at the age of fifty-three whilst working as a cleaner at Haywards Heath train station.

The characters of Epping Forest.

Chapter 9 – Investigating in the Forest

On an unseasonably mild November night in 2022, I decided to make a foray into part of Epping Forest with some friends from the Paracom group (Pete, Melanie, Mark, Keith and newbie Meesha). I had no real plan in place or objectives of what I wanted to do, other than explore one small part of the forest and see what happened. A couple of months prior, I visited another part of the area with my family, and we had been exploring the location of the Old Stump Road (the haunt of highway robbers). Even though it was the middle of the day, at the time, there was no-one else around and I thought I would power up the spirit box and Ovilus and see what happened. The chatter on the P.S.B.7 was evident, there were a couple of distinct voices that sounded like they were having an argument, but I could not make out exactly what they were saying. In a vain attempt to stop my two sons yelling behind me, I asked them to be quiet, when at the same time a very loud female voice came over the radio speaker saying "sssh, silence", uncannily concurrent was the word "silent" on the Ovilus word generator. I am not so naïve that I believe everything that comes through on gadgets, but what was very odd coincidence I felt, although it did spook the children to the point where peace reigned for at least five minutes.

"adults" only…

It was a different part of the woods that I ventured into with the Paracom crew, a couple of them had experienced the unexplained in the woods surrounding the Holy Innocent's church in High Beech, and knowing what I do about that area, I was happy to follow their lead.

As you will probably have realised from other chapters in this book, High Beech as an area, although small, has experienced a lot, but I kept this information from the group as I wanted them to go in cold without any preconceptions and see what they found.

I really am that kind of person...

We started off in the wooded area behind the church, once we had worked out how to get down from the graveyard into the trees anyway. There were some slabs built into the wall for you to step down, although with them covered in slippery wet leaves, no handrail to hold onto, and a few of the team carrying copious amounts of equipment, it was slightly precarious – but I am pleased to report there were no injuries and I am not having to beg, steal or borrow to pay any liability claims! Something I will stress however, is that we were incredibly respectful when walking around, no candles or anything flammable (seriously? Why would you?) and nothing forced or damaged, I genuinely believe that these areas are alive and should be treated with reverence. That attitude which we all held, may have been why later on in the evening we were treated to the sight of some deer, who stood and observed us for quite some time. I was raised in the countryside, so seeing these beautiful creatures in the wild is something I have experienced before - they have even been caught on camera wandering through my parent's garden! But for a couple of the group, it was their first ever encounter and they were quite blown away by it. It did make me think of the legend of the White Stag however, and I was pleased that they were quite definitely deer with colour to their coats and it was Mother nature condoning our visit rather than telling us we were potentially doomed.

Until we got to know what any potential forest energies were most comfortable with, we tried a combination of techniques, ranging from R.E.M. pods to pure and simple calling out, and it came about that the basic gadgets were the best and we gathered some interesting pieces during our night. For any sceptics reading this, I am not saying in any way that they were all spirits trying to communicate, but they were paranormal as we could not explain them.

In the first part of the forest, in a dense thicket a stone's throw from the church, we began. I set a laser grid down on the floor (being very careful not to point it in the sky, whilst it was not an uber-powerful pen, the police helicopter is stationed very close by and was seemingly quite busy that night). Whilst there was a lot of joking around – I'm a big fan of laughter, it really does help the energy levels – Meesha noticed an anomaly regarding the grid that was illuminated by the bright green dots. There was a very distinct area that was blacked out right in the middle of it, almost like a doorway. There was nothing blocking the direction of the device I was using, and the configuration of the lights would not have allowed for that large a gap, so Mark went and placed the R.E.M. pod in the opening in the hope that if it was some kind of paranormal portal, that it would trigger a response. Nature produces many odd sounds that can sound almost ghostly to people who are not used to the area, but what I have never heard before is the sound of a young woman giggling...followed by a loud audible sigh. These are what we heard whilst we were debating on what to do about this laser oddity, to begin with we were asking each other "was that you?" "No, I thought it was you" and then we realised that none of us had made the noises and that maybe we were not alone. I am a big believer in intuition, allowing your mind to wander and become open to external manipulation and that is how I come up with some of the questions I ask when doing E.V.P. sessions and also ideas of what experiments to do.

I tried the P.S.B.7 first. There was distinct chatter, but it was unintelligible and we could not get them to talk more clearly. It reminded me of when I used the device in the nuclear bunker at Kelvedon Hatch, the talking was not interacting with us and it made me wonder if it was picking up some kind of residual energy somehow? It became evident that the spirit box was not going to garner anything, so we switched to something else, trying to communicate via recordings.

As we were doing our first E.V.P. session, I asked a couple of questions: "Did you live in the woods?" "Who was on the throne?" They did not get any response when we played the recording back, but Meesha asked if it was normal to hear a voice that was not her own giving answers in her head. We all encouraged her - as she had never done this before – to embrace it and to tell us what it was telling her, or how it was making her feel, something which is really important when investigating as the human body is still the best piece of equipment you can use. She explained that it was definitely female, young sounding and she could not remember what I had asked just that the responses were no and Henry VIII. Had she connected to the youthful sounding girl whose giggle we had heard? At this point, Mark asked whoever it was to come out from hiding and to come closer, and at that point the R.E.M. pod went off, as though someone had passed through that entrance in the trees.

I will admit to asking Meesha first if she was willing to undertake a bit of an adventure for me, and whether she would go and stand in the space that the laser was not hitting. Being a fearless teenager, she went straight over there, and the photo that Mark captured was very strange; whilst we were not aiming at transmogrification, her face changed. She also (despite the ground being level) looked about seven feet tall. We then asked Pete to go and stand in the same place, his face seemed to alter as well – pretty sure it was not Mark's camera as he is quite the tech person – but when a person's wife (Pete's better half Melanie was also on the investigation) looks at the photo and exclaims that it is not her husband, you get the impression that something a bit odd is going on.

Whilst neither of them said that they felt particularly odd when standing there, they definitely acted differently, even though they were only twenty feet or so away. Their attention wandered and you had to repeat yourself more than once to get them to respond. I will admit that it was quite intriguing and something I did not expect, leading me to wonder whether Epping Forest has some kind of spiritual portal?

It started to get me thinking who this young woman who had latched onto us was, and did she use the woods as some kind of refuge from life? We know that Henry VIII spent time there, after all it was for him that the Great Standing at Chingford (now known as Queen Elizabeth Hunting Lodge) was erected, and he was well known to love hunting.

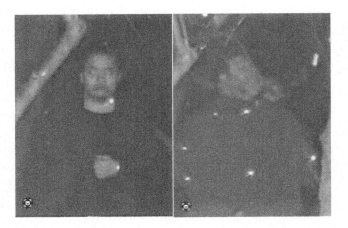

Photos of both Meesha and Pete, the spots on them are the laser grid, both of them have had their face shapes changed standing there.

I said that I had this image of a young woman who looked different to others in my mind and that was why both Meesha and Pete were having their faces altered to look flatter and rounder - was she bullied because of her appearance and sought salvation in the woods of Epping? It has to be said that Meesha said she felt someone pushing into her back as I was explaining my thoughts and that to her, I was spot on. In order to help this spirit, I suggested Meesha walk over to the portal and tell her she could hold her hand, so she could sense that not all people are cruel and taunting. The youngest member of the team did say that she felt a weight in her hand, and whilst it did feel like someone was holding it in the truest sense, that something was pulling on it and would not stop. By asking the spirit to let go, the pressure ceased, and we decided to run another quick E.V.P, the question being "do you want us to stay here." A female voice came back with "keep moving." Okay then.

That was further compounded by Mark saying to knock twice if they wanted us to move on, two sharp bangs were heard in direct response.

Mark really wanted to find this body of water that he had been told by friends had produced a lot of activity when they were beside it. I have to admit to being reluctant knowing what I do about the forest and its connection with water-based deaths – not to mention that it was very dark and going paddling was not on my list of things to do that evening.

We eventually found the pond that he had wanted to find, although the sat-nav feature on the phone kept leading us in weird directions, following the compass in the direction it told us to go, and then suddenly it was behind us, or to the left when it had originally been on the right. Saying that, it was remarkably inactive, in fact, the spookiest thing was listening to what sounded like someone being attacked, two of us in the group identified it as being foxes mating. I will admit though that the longer the screaming went on (and an audio version of pareidolia did almost make it sound like "help me" was being said) I started to wonder if we were right and whether we should go and check. It definitely gave an eerie atmosphere to the forest at that point, but it was about as spooky as the area got as nothing happened at all.

Actually, that is not strictly true, something did happen - one of the team had the most terrifying experience in his life, one that reduced the rest of us into useless, hysterical children. Keith (the person who took all the full spectrum pictures with his adapted Go Pro that I believe is so precious, it has its own bedroom back home) had brought a fur-lined flying hat to wear when it got cold. Due to the unseasonal mildness, he had taken it off and shoved it in his pocket with the fur lining poking out slightly. As we started walking back to the Church, we heard him scream and shout that something had touched him, obviously being concerned colleagues we stopped to check he was okay and then he uttered the words that caused the laughter to flow uncontrollably:

"Oh, don't worry, it was just my hat."

It transpires that he had totally forgotten where he had put it, and his hand brushed the fur part as he was walking, and he thought something unconsented had caressed his hand. I did warn him that it was going in the book as it was too good not to, it is not that often that something reduces you into such a jointless mess that you are laughing so hard your ribs hurt.

Making our way back to where we had parked up outside the church for a drink and a biscuit (got to keep those sugar levels up), we were leaning against our cars, but only two of us were facing the church. As we were all chatting about what we were going to do next, myself and one other saw a shadow flash past the main church door, we both saw it in real time, but it was what was to happen next that really added to the experience.

Deciding to stand on the concrete behind the building and away from the graves, Meesha and I wandered off to work out the best place, but the others did not follow us. Making our way back to them, they had their ears up against the same door that I had seen the apparition move past ten minutes beforehand, they could hear noise inside, almost like footsteps on the stone floor. Whilst we could not get any other responses (although the Ovilus did say 'work' and 'brass'…was somebody polishing or brass rubbing?) the interaction around the back was interesting and gave us a few E.V.Ps.

Taken by the church, no smudge on the lens or people breathing (or vaping) (picture by Mark)

The spirit box was not generating anything, neither was the necrophonic app, so we went to good old-fashioned E.V.P. and calling out, Pete asked how many spirits were with them, and whilst there was no vocal reply picked up, there is a definite tap tap tap in direct response, maybe this person could not count? I asked my favourite question, was it a King or Queen on the throne, listening back at the time we thought we heard a faint voice say Queen, but on playing back and clearing out some of the background noise there are two different responses to my question, Queen and then someone with what sounds like a stutter trying to get the word Queen out as well. It can also be described as a weird sensation we had while standing there that we were being watched and circled. More than once on the recordings you can hear someone (living, not a spirit) ask who moved? Or who is behind me? And no-one is...it was almost as though they were nervous to come too close as they were not used to anyone wanting to communicate with them.

Following on from my King or Queen question, I asked if they could tell us the name of the monarch. Whilst the response is not really worthy of much, there was upon listening back to the recording, a whispered response although despite trying my best, I cannot clear it up enough to be intelligible.

After the church, we ventured back into a different part of the woods. Now, for this part, I want to refer you to my chapter on Buildings of the Forest of Essex, specifically Riggs Retreat – you will understand why shortly. Mark had investigated this specific sector before, and had been accompanied by a psychic medium, who had apparently said the area was full of soldiers running around. Had I been there at the time – our little gang did not have a medium – I would probably have quizzed them on the uniforms they were wearing, as I know that the run up to the First World War, and in the early years, soldiers were based at Riggs Retreat in High Beech and were training in the woods. Even before that, they would sometimes spend a short while at the Kings Oak, and even prior to that, local memories of many soldiers who came through the forest on foot and horseback after the Boer War (Keepers, Cockneys and Kitchen Maids – Georgina Green, page 10) so even in the last hundred and fifty years, the woods and military have links. Again, the spirit box did not seem to be working very well, and we resorted to the R.E.M. pod and the necrophonic app. Whilst the pod did not yield any results, some interesting words were coming through the word generator and whilst I am not in any way suggesting that it is fool proof, they were certainly interesting.

I did not tell the others about the history of service people in the woods, and especially the area of High Beech, until after the investigation had finished so as not to influence what they were hearing on the app. Words like soldier, war, weapon, fight were all clearly discernible but it was the repeated use of "fire" that was interesting – to me at least, knowing what I did. The other funny part was that they seemed to still be on operations in between the trees. It reminded me of that story of Japanese Second World War soldier, Hiro Onoda, who was based in Lubang in the Philippines just before the Americans attacked it, but he stayed not realising the war had been lost and stayed on his mission of protecting the island. He did not return to Japan for thirty years, having been declared dead by the authorities fifteen years earlier. It was always joked by my family that had I joined the military, I would have been an officer - are they trying to say I like ordering people about? So, I put on my best authoritative voice and said "all soldiers, back to base camp, get some scran." That produced a response from the word app as well, I think it sounded like 'understood' but there was definitely a 'Bye'.

Whilst we assumed at the time that "fire" was to do with guns, I wonder if it was to do more with the catastrophic fire that destroyed Riggs in 1916. As I always do, I thanked the forest and its resident energies for their time and giving so much to us. There were lots of noises that could have been paranormal, could have been footsteps but as I cannot confirm indefinitely that they were, I have excluded them from this account and only written about the things that seemed to directly correlate with what we were doing at the time.

Another day, another exploration.

I mentioned in an earlier chapter about the poltergeist of Warren Hill woods, who back in 1908 had apparently been lobbing missiles at people who used the cut-through to get from Chingford to Loughton, and I made the decision to find it, and see if anyone wanted to try that with me. Even I am not brave enough to go into the woods, in the middle of a suburban area at night on my own – trust me, it is not the deceased that I am afraid of – so instead, a few pleasant hours with the family wandering about some beautiful, forested area was just the tonic (plus it got the children away from their electronics and breathing some fresh air).

We parked up just near Oaklands School on the Loughton side and picked the footpath that led us straight through to Manor Road and passed parallel to the A104. The main purpose was to explore rather than gather any paranormal information, but you should never look a gift horse in the mouth as they say, and I was equipped with a few gadgets that may (or may not) pick anything up whilst combining exercising both children and dog. My eldest son is a budding investigator in the making, and I am training him to be both respectful and courteous. I have probably said this before in previous work, but I think there is nothing wrong with responsible children communicating with spirit as long as they are supervised and are not going to be scared when something does happen. Fortunately, my eldest son has grown up with it, and has had experiences since he was very small. He is also aware that what you see on some of the You Tube videos is a load of codswallop and that people who run around screaming and yelling "demons" are not how it is done by the majority of investigators and researchers.

The Elements of Epping Forest

He had asked to help, so I gave him the K2 to hold whilst we traversed the length of the forest. It was only half a mile or so and I was running my Ovilus and spirit box - stupidly I had not checked that the external speaker had been charged up, so I had to rely on the incredibly quiet unit itself and kept it pretty much glued to my ear. From the minute I switched it on there was chatter, despite my setting the sweep to the fastest possible, and the voices were the same, a woman, a man and a younger- sounding voice who seemed to interject every so often, but I could not make out what they were saying.

As we were coming up the slight incline to Manor Road, the K2 shot to red and stayed there, at which point (eldest son was getting very excited), I thanked the spirit and asked them to step away from the lights. Straight away it went back down to green – cue big grins between son and I, and also exclamations of gratitude from both of us. The test would be to see if we could get it to light up again; by this point my younger son was asking questions as well, it seems that the combined energy of two interested children was giving the spirits enough to communicate.

And yes, we did manage to get the K2 to go up to red again when we asked them to come back towards us.

The next interesting thing after we crossed the road to the next bit of forest was the P.S.B.7 activity. There were direct answers to our questions on that, as my eldest said he heard a young person's voice coming through saying "hello", the word "child" came up on the Ovilus. I introduced myself, and asked if they could repeat my name if they were able, and then "Penny" was heard through the white noise. I asked where we were, and we heard a reply almost instantly of a male voice, but we could not work out what it said, although "wood" came up on the word generator, and then "November". At one point, my youngest had a temper tantrum and would not walk properly back towards our car as he was getting tired as there are quite a few inclines to walk up and down

– straight away the spirit box male voice said "well, leave." That was us told. I did scold the youngest for not walking properly, and he shouted at me for pushing him, when the same male voice told us to "stop." We were definitely being scolded for arguing. We reached the beautifully spooky tree and the boys sat down for a rest, the youngest worrying that he had upset the spirits of the forest and he apologised and asked them to forgive his outburst. "Sorry" came over the airwaves very audibly. As we were about to leave the area, I said thank you and goodbye to whoever/whatever had been communicating with us, and we all heard "bye" from the device. I am sceptical of so much interaction in such a short space of time, but there were two adult witnesses, and a thirteen-year-old child who can testify to all of it, so sometimes it just happens!

Definitely a place to re-visit, if not just for the beautiful, ancient trees, many of whom descend from its time as the centre of Henry VIII's deer park in the 16th century.

Chapter 10 – Buildings of the forest

It is inevitable that an area as huge as that which we term Epping Forest (although for the sake of being totally accurate, I am including Waltham Forest and Hainault into the all-encompassing coverall) would have some interesting buildings that we can discuss. Many of these are not available to paranormal investigators (at the time of writing anyway), but it does not mean that you cannot visit them, understand their history and appreciate what was once there.

One of the reasons I began Haunted Histories in the first place was to examine some of the historical claims that people made about places, and whether they had any grain of truth to them. In most cases that grain is non-existent, or at the very least incredibly questionable, which leads me to the first place I am going to cover, the Kings Oak Hotel in High Beech. This is a very large, licensed venue in the heart of the forest, very popular with ramblers and cyclists alike (I do wonder if they know the irony of that, but more later), and behind it is one of the Epping visitor centres which I would recommend visiting for information about the location.

I had discovered whilst searching through the archives at Essex Records Office that the hotel had the accolade of being the location of the first ever motorcycle speedway track in Britain. In fact, you can see the original designs for the whole facility which was built by W.J. Cearns Builders (whose letter head grandly states that they are

War Office Contractors). The Grandstand was to have fourteen different levels, but that was not all that the drawings showed. They accounted for a car park for spectators and competitors alike, a hotel, baths, washhouses, plumbed toilets and a sloping track which was three-hundred and sixty-three yards on the inside. The first actual event on this cinder track was held on the 19th February 1928, and hundreds of people turned up to watch, crowding into both the inside and outside parts of the track not being used by the riders – there is a report saying that people even climbed into the trees to get a better view!

Now whilst this is very much the truth, the account I read of Henry VIII's involvement with Kings Oak is very doubtful. Whilst researching for this chapter, I was looking at history blogs that have been written about the area. They can be useful for looking into pieces and finding reference material, but this one said that the Kings Oak Hotel was where said Tudor King waited until he heard confirmation of Anne Boleyn's execution on 19th May 1536. This seemed slightly confusing to me, firstly even though High Beech is only twelve miles from London, it is still a fair way to travel. Also the hotel itself is Victorian, so would not have existed back then. I looked in all the Tudor era chronicles that I could find but could not see any notes as to what Henry was doing that day (other than the fact that on the 20th May, he was betrothed to wife number three, Jane Seymour). Luckily, many historians are a friendly bunch, and Nathen Amin shared my question for me on social media, and the brilliant Dr. Tracy Borman came back with an answer – he was at Whitehall until he heard the canons go off to signify his wife's death and then travelled by river to his Chelsea manor house to see Jane Seymour.

That is not to say he did not travel to the forest at Epping, but the Kings Oak is not named as such because of Henry's involvement with it. Far more likely is another explanation given, which goes even further back in time to that of the Battle of Hastings and King Harold. The former King had strong links with the area, his family owned a local manor and he had helped fund the rebuilding of the abbey in 1060 – which is why he is commemorated there and many believe is interred in the grounds too. Old postcards from the 19th century show a crumbling old oak tree, little more than a stump, next to the much more grand, wide leafed beauty planted for Queen Victoria in 1882 and it stands right in front of the hotel. Sometimes you do not need to be a detective to find the most obvious answer.

The Kings Oak as an establishment had a variety of owners and proprietors during the period from the latter 1800s to the 1930s, and they certainly seemed to be a mixed bunch from a behavioural point of view.

Looking at newspaper adverts from the 19th century, the first landlord mentioned is Joseph Elves, who had formerly been the proprietor of the White Lion in Hackney Wick and had moved out to the forest with his wife and nine children. Tragically, it seems that Esther (his spouse) died in the second half of 1881 at the young age of forty-five, and only five years later, the children lost their father at the ridiculously early age of fifty.

By the time of Joseph's passing, the pub was owned by a man who went by the name of Christopher William Pfleger. I cannot say gentleman - the information I will give you shortly is going to explain why in very specific detail.

It seems that in April 1882, Pfleger took on the license and then the drama started. A cursory glance of the newspapers from the period of 1882 to 1887 (when he moved on to another establishment) was nothing but accounts of assault, fighting and incredibly bad feeling. In that era, many barmaids lived in the place they worked, and part of their weekly salary included board, as was the case with Alice Sutton. Just a month or so after the new landlord was in place, he told her that she was sacked. Now Ms. Sutton was aware of her rights and said that he had to give her notice for not only was this her job, but also where she lived. According to the subsequent court records – and I am paraphrasing here slightly, but you get the gist – he told her that he did not care and that he wanted her out. When Pfleger came back from going to Epping market he found Alice still in the establishment and proceeded to throw her onto the land outside, injuring her to the point that she had to get medical assistance. This is where I admire this woman - she took him to court, and won, being awarded the two weeks' pay that she was due and also a month in lieu of notice.

I do think that the landlord of the Kings Oak either had a real temper problem, enjoyed the publicity (he would probably have been a social media star for all the wrong reasons in the world of today) or he was just a total and utter piece of work, but the account I found from September 1885 was enough to make my blood boil.

Yes, I know historians should stay unbiased, but if you do not growl at the page after reading what I am about to tell you, then we need to have words.

On 15th August 1885, Eliza Pfleger had applied to the Hendon Poor Board for relief as she had been unable to find work and was destitute. These institutions did not pay out or offer a place in the Workhouse without investigation and found out that Eliza was actually married to the landlord of the Kings Oak Hotel in High Beech. Yes, the very same volatile and obnoxious man mentioned above. They wrote to him, because in those days it was the husband's responsibility to pay for his wife and children (if he was able) and he and Eliza had produced four children during their marriage. After ten days he had not responded, so she was allowed into the Workhouse and he was summoned to court for not meeting his duties as a husband.

His estranged wife testified that she had left him four and half years previously because he was abusive, and she and her daughters were unable to live with him any longer. The last straw for her had been him threatening to blow her brains out whilst aiming a gun at her, although I would have thought another statement where she said he would chase her and their daughters through the house with a large carving knife was bad enough. She also said that he would evict her from their marital bed and bring home other women, one of which he was now living with at Kings Oak and ignoring his fiscal responsibilities as a father. Of course, as with so many of these types of spouses, he denied all of it and said that in their previous pub (before he took on the Kings Oak) she had been having an affair with a dance teacher they had employed to teach evening classes and had also stolen furniture when she left him. If that was not bad enough, he implied that she "fraternised" with the patrons of the pub and would frequently stay up drinking with them after he had retired to bed. It seems that he had not bargained on the appearance of his son, or his daughters in court. They all corroborated their mother's statement and also added more...she only socialised with the customers when he made her (was he pimping her out to the clientele? One has to wonder) and if dinner was not to his liking, he would lob a leg of mutton at her head, or throw hot tea in her face in anger.

I did have to chuckle when I saw that the court found unanimously in Eliza's favour and ordered that he pay her twenty shillings a week – unsurprisingly he said he would appeal.

You may think a bully like Pfleger would have learned his lesson, since these women were prepared to stand up to him in a court of law, but no, he still went searching for trouble and being somewhat antagonistic. On 30th May 1886, there was a quasi "riot" at the Hotel, coach loads of young men travelled down from central London and when he tried to stop them playing on the swings in the grounds of the hotel – this place covered around six acres, and had stabling for at least eighty horses, it was huge – they turned on him, and he was injured quite badly (although not before trying to shoot them). It went to court as you would expect, but for some reason was thrown out...the judge seemed to believe that he had caused some of the issues and that the young men would not have retaliated like that if he had not.

In January 1887, he passed the license on to another person, something which the courts were very happy about as they said: "The place had been a regular nuisance to the neighbourhood and the bench had had more trouble with it than any other house in the division".

In March 1888, the license was passed over to George Ludwig Gumprecht, a German who had resided in England for decades by that point, although he certainly seemed to be met with suspicion as the court tried very hard to block his application for the Oak and said that the house would be closely watched – I have to wonder if the same comments were made about non-German licensees? Articles mention him as "Herr" Gumprecht, the Teutonic landlord and various other terms which one could quite easily view as xenophobic. However, to George's credit, he certainly seemed to turn the prejudice on its head. In 1891 he constructed the cycling and athletic track which was to be used eventually for the ground-breaking speedway track just under forty years later. Various cycling and rambling groups started to frequent the hotel for food and relaxation and was used as a base for many individuals who were using the forest for whatever purpose they chose. Whether it was for the London Rifle Brigade camping out nearby in May 1895, or the local gymkhana, stabling for horses or just the annual meeting of the licensed victuallers, Gumprecht seemed to turn the place around (although he did get in trouble once, for allowing his dog to roam the forest unmuzzled).

In 1908 he sadly died, the same year that probably the biggest scandal hit the hotel when a barmaid, Jennie Palmer, was found guilty of attempted suicide after trying to drown herself in nearby Connaught Waters. She had been incredibly depressed at the fact that her husband was unable to find work, but the courts released her into his care with her assurances that she would not try this again.

After Gumprecht Senior passed away, his son Ludwig took over the running of the establishment, and he certainly seemed to operate with the same morals and ethics of his father, although that did not mean he did not face opposition from locals. Shortly after the outbreak of World War One, there was a lot of anti-German feeling pervading the British psyche, and even though Gumprecht was born and bred (and proven) British, he still had to defend himself and his heritage. It cannot be a coincidence that in September 1914, a huge fire blazed its way through the outbuildings of his hotel and could have done very serious damage to the forest itself, had it not been for the incredibly quick thinking of the residents and fire service to stop it.

Much was subsequently made of the proprietor's devotion to his home country, after all, who would allow his three sons to all go to the front to fight against the "enemy" if you were secretly a sympathiser? Tragically, and as happened to so many families, he lost his son Ernest at the age of just twenty-one, fighting in Ypres, and he is commemorated on the Menin Gate. One of his other sons wrote home in June 1915, talking about the amazing men of the flying corps and how no-one could compete with the British rapid rifle fire. He also mentioned having seen a Zeppelin brought down by an aviator who was awarded a Victoria Cross for his bravery. I decided to dig a bit deeper to try and work out who that was, and stumbled upon the tale of Reginald Warneford, who had joined the Royal Naval Air Service, and on the 7th June 1915, dropped an airborne bomb on LZ-37, which was on its way over Ostend. What Gumprecht's son would not have been aware of however was even though the V.C. was awarded to Warneford, he was left off the list because he had been born in India and not Britain. The pilot died just ten days after his record-breaking exploits when on a publicity flight. The struts on his aircraft broke, causing the wings to fold up and the airplane plummeted to the ground.

You may be interested to know that he did ultimately receive his medal, and it is displayed at the Fleet Air Arm Museum.

There is much more you can learn about Kings Oak, but I will leave it there for now...go walking or cycling in the forest and you will most probably stumble across it. If you do not want to go in the pub itself, there is a lovely café adjoining the building, along with the forest visitor centre just behind, which is a bevy of information and insight into the forest, both its history and its fauna.

Riggs Retreat

Many people with psychic abilities have picked up on soldiers in the forest, and especially the High

Beech area, but why? We know that in the late 19th century, the London Rifle Brigade did training in the area, but these images are described as the khaki uniforms, and more akin to that worn in the first world war as opposed to earlier ones.

I may have an answer…of sorts.

The next location we will cover is one called Riggs Retreat.

These were large buildings where people could obtain non-alcoholic refreshments whilst enjoying the clean, pure air of the forest. Riggs created four of these sites: High Beech, Theydon Bois, Buckhurst Hill and one at Clacton. One can only imagine the thousands of visitors from the East End of London who came to visit. In 1881, William Riggs (the son of the original Riggs) opened the centre at Wellington Hill in High Beech and there begins our story.

The train line from London had reached Loughton by 1856 and Chingford by 1873, combine that with enterprising local businessmen providing horse drawn brakes (a coach if you will) to bring families out to the woods and greenery for a day of fun, and sixteen-hour days for those working in these retreats was not unusual for the March to September period. If you think about it, how many people chose to escape to these kinds of areas during the Covid 19 lockdown we experienced in 2020? I guess a temporary liberation from the smoke and noise of East London was not such a different feeling of rejuvenation.

Soldiers Penny, Soldiers! You said you had an idea about the military sightings…and that I do, I am setting a scene here for you.

So, William married the daughter of the local publican who ran the nearby Robin Hood pub (which is still there, but is now a Thai restaurant) Angelique Chilton, in 1886. By the 1891 census they were living at Riggs Retreat in High Beech with two children, running the business together. William went off to fight in the Boer War and was one of the men given the South African war medal at Horse Guards Parade by the King, although it may have been the dance thrown at his retreat by his wife at the same point in August to celebrate his safe return that had meant more.

At the outbreak of the First World War in 1914, William tried to enlist into the military, but he was well over fifty years old by this point, so unsurprisingly even with his Boer War experience, he was said to be too old – the maximum age was forty-one for conscription. He was instead, placed in the catering corps, and his experience at having run Riggs for so many years, would have stood him in good stead. The other thing about his retreat was that it was located at Wellington Hill, the highest point in the forest, so was utilised by the early balloon divisions who were there to try and counter the German zeppelins coming over the water. Not only that, the buildings were requisitioned to be a training base for the Artists Rifles, the Bankers Battalion and some other groups of soldiers.

The Artists Rifles were quite an old unit, created in 1859. They were made up of many people with (as the name would suggest) an artistic background, but by W.W.1, predominantly private school and university graduates, and became a training ground for officers. You may even have heard some of the names such as Wilfred Owen and Noel Coward. I cannot say whether either of these trained in Epping Forest, but they certainly wore the uniform. This battalion proved so popular to join, that by the year 1900 it had twelve companies (so one-hundred and fifty men in each) but by 1914, it had been divided into three sub battalions.

Another name I mentioned, the Bankers Battalion, was not formed until 1915 and also went by the name 26th Royal Fusiliers. Their war history mentions battles that even the person who only has a rudimentary knowledge of the Great War would have heard of: The Somme, Messines Ridge, Menin Road…they would have seen some awful death and destruction. It must have been a sight to see all these soldiers marching from the forest to the train stations at Loughton and Chingford for their onward journey to the front.

Whilst many may not find what happened early in the morning on Sunday 17th September 1916 unusual – especially as this building was of wooden construction and had no gas or electricity (paraffin lamps and coal for cooking were the order of the day) – burned to the ground. Many articles say how the fire brigade were unable to save the building as by the time they got there, the blaze had taken such a strong hold that the bigger risk was it spreading into the forest. Thankfully their brave work stopped that happening, although some of the trees nearby did get damaged by the flames. I am sure the destruction of what was to many, a form of sanctuary from the hustle, bustle and pollution of London, would have caused great sadness. Riggs was not the only retreat in the forest back then, and you can still visit one now - Butlers Retreat in Chingford - in fact, pop in for a cup of coffee and then you can go and explore my next building.

Queen Elizabeth Hunting Lodge – photos by author.

Most people are aware of Henry VIII's penchant for hunting, it was most definitely a Tudor sport as they had restored some of the forest which a charter of King John (confirmed by Edward IV) had been reduced. Even during the early part of his life, there were at least three hunting lodges in the forest of Essex, and Henry (assume I mean VIII and not his father) certainly pursued this hobby until the last years of his life – there are reports of him being hoisted into the saddle by a mechanical device when he was too obese and lacking in mobility to mount his horse himself. He acquired Chingford Earl in 1541 and Chingford St. Pauls in 1544, but between those dates, had commissioned George Maxey to construct the three-floor, very grand "Great Stonedeings" (Great Standing) for £30 (about £18,000 in today's money) in his new park at "Fayremeade", known more commonly now as Fairmead. Henry is believed to have had over two-hundred hunting lodges, although that is perhaps not surprising since he also owned over fifty-five palaces, so indulgence and displays of his wealth were not unusual. It was there to protect the "vert" and hunt venison, the latter meaning wild game in general and not just deer.

The Great Standing that was originally built for people to watch the hunt from would have had a totally open structure, and the floors were slanted to allow rain to drain away. After Henry passed away and his properties eventually passed to his younger daughter Elizabeth, she is said to have also enjoyed these pursuits, and strongly advocated being active in general. A letter she is said to have sent to the Earl of Rutland said:

Her Majesty desires that you should remember her request to you which was that you should indever to perfecte your healthe with exercise, and smeth she knoeth you are lyke her in that she is not delighted with enye sport much, yet for thealth sake, and because you shall plese her therin, she would you should enfore yourselfe to such exercyses as agree with you.

We know that she visited the forest on occasion, she spent five days in May 1578 at Wanstead House, owned then by her close friend Robert Dudley, Earl of Leicester – this was about four months before he married his second wife, Lettice Knollys who was a cousin of the Queen and incurred her jealousy. Whilst there is no proof she visited Fairmead park to hunt during this stay, it is believed highly likely.

Another interesting tale (and I do hope it is true) was that the Queen, upon hearing of the defeat of the Spanish Armada in 1588, rode her horse up the internal staircase of the lodge to celebrate. The stairs are not that difficult to traverse, but I am not sure if I would want to ride my horse up them, although bringing it back down would probably be the trickier aspect of the whole thing.

Elizabeth must have held the building in high regard for in 1589, she commissioned a survey to assess its condition and any repairs it may need. The report indicates that by this point it had been enclosed.

After Elizabeth passed the throne to James I, he still carried on using the lodge for hunting and we know that by 1777, it was being recognised as "Queen Elizabeth Hunting Lodge" due to maps from that particular era naming it thus. Its next role in life was as the manorial court from the mid-17th century to around 1851, not so much because it gave off a sense of gravitas as that specific type of judiciary justice was the lowest around, but more so that the upkeep would have been the responsibility of the Lord of the manor, who also presided over the court and the forest.

As a quick tourist type history plug, it is well worth a visit if you are in the area, and even better…it is free!

I would like to take you on a brief tangent if I may - next door to this hunting lodge is a hotel, the Royal Forest to be precise, and whilst you will hear it mentioned in at least one other chapter in this book, I thought I would give you a bit of its backstory. The Forest Hotel commenced construction in 1879 and was renamed the Royal Forest Hotel after Queen Victoria's visit to the forest and her gift of it to the people. It was placed there to cater for the masses of tourists who chose to visit the area and to cater for those wishing to stay a little longer.

On the 14th May 1912 however, a huge blaze rampaged its way through the resort, destroying thirty- five of the sixty-five bedrooms and severely damaged the rest. The rebuild of the hotel was without the fourth storey which had originally been there. The current owners, Brewers Fayre, say that they believe it is haunted, and that two guests and a fireman perished in the blaze. With me being the kind of person I am, I started to research that possibility – not of a haunting, as hotels do see death anyway, even without external factors such as huge fires – but of three people dying on the 14th May 1912.

My first port of call were the newspapers. I went through various searches: the fire, the hotel, fireman deaths, and none produced an answer confirming that anyone lost their life, in fact quite the opposite, they stated that it was amazing that there were no fatalities. By 1912, all deaths had to be recorded by law, so I looked at the register in respect of anyone who died in the second quarter of the year, and was aged between 16 and 65 to see if any could be attributed to the fire.

I drew a negative there as well, so if anyone reading this has the actual details of the identities of these people (if indeed there were any), please do let me know.

The next location does segue into this one quite easily, a beautiful hall which also had Queen Elizabeth I grace it with her presence.

Copped Hall

Christine Matthews / Copped Hall, Essex / CC BY-SA 2.0 wikipedia

This beautiful building (not to be confused with the former Copped Hall in Totteridge) has had some kind of construction on the site since at least the 13th century, however the hall you see now is Georgian and was built in the 1740s when John Conyers inherited it from his late father.

Before I continue with this tale which involves the following: the Tower of London, one of the most internationally famous haunted places in the world along with fire, impeachment and famous pop stars, I will say that the trust that now owns this property and is looking to restore it for educational purposes does not embrace paranormal investigations, so unless you get a kick out of rejection, do not approach them (www.coppedhalltrust.org.uk) but if you want to learn more about its history, then go along to one of their open days.

In the 12ᵗʰ century, during the reign of Henry II, two acres of forest was allocated for hunting, and a lodge was established. The theme of nobles hunting is definitely one which pervades the forest, and the family who were responsible for it during this time were the Fitzauchers. It was licensed in 1293, and ten years later upon the death of Henry Fitzaucher comprised a total of one-hundred and eighty acres – with a mixture of meadow land, park and arable.

Just to illustrate how powerful the various Abbeys around the country were (and possibly why Henry VIII eventually saw them as a rich source of funds to plunder), in March 1350, the owner Sir John Shardlow, exchanged it for other lands (the Manor of Boreham, and grounds in Cambridgeshire) with the Abbots of Waltham. In 1537, the Abbots were persuaded to give the Hall and its lands to King Henry VIII in a vain attempt to save their Abbey - probably no surprise to know that this generous gift was not any help, and Waltham Abbey was dissolved on 23ʳᵈ March 1540. A Little fact for you, Waltham was the last Abbey to suffer this fate (although not the last monastery) which historians and scholars believe was due to the Kings fondness for the place. We know he visited Essex on a regular basis and is said to have frequented this particular abbey for long conversations with the Abbot.

This is when things start to get a bit juicier…after Henry VIII died, his son Edward VI took over. He seemed to be a bit more lenient towards his older sister and granted Mary (the future Queen) the right to live in Copped Hall. She had an entourage helping her manage her house, and one of those was the trusted Sir Edward Waldegrave. By 1551, Edward (he was not knighted until 1553), had been working for Mary some four years, but her little brother the King imprisoned him in the Tower of London for refusing to stop his mistress saying Mass in Copped Hall. He was held there for about a year and when Mary became Queen in 1553, he received his Knighthood, was appointed to the Privy Council and also allocated various other Manors. Unfortunately, his Catholicism was going to be his downfall in the end, as around a year after Queen Mary's death in 1558, with his refusal to stop saying Mass in his home, Queen Elizabeth had him sent to the Tower again, and he died in 1561, still a prisoner. This is where the link to one of the most famous haunted places in the world lies, and no, I do not mean the infamous Tower of London, for Edward was born in Borley, Essex and in the very same church which originally sat next to the notorious Borley Rectory. So strong were his links to this part of North Essex, that there is a fourteen-foot-high tomb and memorial to Sir Edward and his wife Frances.

Elizabeth I had already given the manor to a personal favourite of hers, Sir Thomas Heneage in 1564, by 1625 it had been sold to Sir Lionel Cranfield and was where he spent his years following his impeachment. I did say things were going to get interesting. One sees the word "impeachment" and assumes that the person is guilty, although with Cranfield I would say it was not the case. He had a meteoric rise through the royal courts, having been introduced to James I at the age of thirty in 1605, knighted in 1613, M.P.

for Hythe in 1614 and Lord High Treasurer by 1621. Part of his problem was that he was incredibly astute when it came to finances, and he could see that the King was spending far too much money and had two choices - either restrict the Kings spending (not good) or increase the Kings revenue. To do this, he introduced a raft of reforms including reduced pension payments, debts to the Crown having to be repaid and increased rents on Crown properties. The issue was that this made him enemies with some incredibly powerful people including George Villiers, the Duke of Buckingham. He was arrested for corruption and bribery, and although only imprisoned for a few days, ostracised from court.

The hall passed through other hands until the current Georgian property was established, and the next dramatic event (although there were undoubtedly others during those one-hundred and fifty years that I have just bypassed) was the First World War. There are some accounts that say the doors of the hall were thrown open (like so many others) to look after wounded soldiers from the battlefields, however I cannot find any documented evidence of that at the time of writing this. Although, the son of John Conyers (who rebuilt the hall in the 1700s) was John Conyers II, and he is credited as creating the 1st Essex Yeomanry in 1797. He is also listed as being complicit in the horrific slave trade by "owning" people on the island of St. Kitts.

Anyway, it is said that fire is a cleanser, which is perhaps why early in the morning of the 6th May 1917, a blaze started in one of the upstairs bedrooms and soon took hold, gutting the building and forced the family to move into a nearby house on the estate. There were many reasons for the disaster bandied about (including a servant dropping an errant cigarette whilst watching the Zeppelin raids on nearby London from the roof) but the more likely reason is simply an electrical fault.

I mentioned a link to pop stars as well? Rod Stewart lived in the manor house there for quite some time and even built his own five-a-side football pitch in the grounds.

So, there you go, some buildings of the forest. There are of course many more, too numerous to cover in this book, but hopefully this gives you a bit of an idea as to the versatility of the area.

Chapter 11 – The forest in fiction

I am not surprised that Epping Forest has been immortalised in fiction on more than one occasion, and I thought you might be interested to know about a few of them.

There are quite a few books and poems I could draw on that talk about the forest, even without mentioning it by name, but I have narrowed it down to five books that I am going to give you a brief synopsis of. I have varied the theme of each novel so that you can see just how versatile the area is. We have horror, historical fiction, fantasy historical, classic and crime. There was a book written by William Addison in 1945 called *"Epping Forest – Its Literary and Historical Associations"* which I will be referring to at points, but not directly as it is an appraisal of some of the writings related to the forest and not a novel which uses the area as its setting.

The first one that I am going to focus on probably did for the forest, what the film "Jaws" did for swimming in the sea, and if it did not have the same reaction, it can only be because not that many people read the second part of the series that horror writer James Herbert wrote about the rodent that seems to terrify people more than any other, the rat.

Whilst the first book *"The Rats"* is set predominantly in the East End of London with vivid descriptions of the bomb-damaged slum-like aftermath of the Second World War, rife with hiding places for these huge, hybrid creatures, the second book moves out of that area and further afield. *'Lair'* begins straight away in the idyllic and bucolic setting of Epping Forest, although the first resident to be featured is a farmer with a vermin problem - obvious foreshadowing of what is to come. We all know that the fun images of a family playing, a young girl making friends with a "doggy" is meant to lure us either into a false sense of security or make us yell at Herbert to leave the child alone, whilst a horse bolting when sensing something deep in the woodland whilst on patrol with a forest keeper is a strong hint that something nefarious is lurking beneath the beautiful greenery.

I am unashamedly a fan of James Herbert's writing, he was a creator of what I called plausible horror - things that could be lurking in the shadows or behind closed doors or even in plain sight and were not as far-fetched as some may think – after all, there are many scientists who believe rats could be the dominant species if there was an extinction event to hit humanity. It is the way that he describes the forest as a living, breathing being that makes you realise that it is as much a character in the book as the main hero, Luke Pender. Early on when Pender goes to visit the conservation centre to speak with Jenny she says (p.56):

"Can't you feel it? The forest – the forest is standing still." - Pender's response is that at first it puzzles him, but he begins to feel it too, all the normal sounds of a wood hushed, no birds chattering, no scampering of the more timid animals and even no breeze hissing through the trees, the forest had stopped breathing.

This is an effect I have been told about before, at places of extreme horror such as Auschwitz, where there are no normal noises of nature, as though the evil pervading the soil has rendered them mute.

To add to how the forest provides, he also stresses how big the population is who lives in it, and also that there are multiple areas – it is not one giant wooded area, there are communities everywhere, not to mention a variety of needs being met by the northern equator's version of a jungle. There are myriad supporting casts whose day (and night) revolve around the forest, some more salubrious than others. The result of the threat of the giant rats and the terror that the storyteller created meant that one character (Jan), always wary of the forest and seeing it's darkness as fearful as opposed to relaxing, felt that "Epping Forest had rapidly lost all its charm" (p.139). The question is however, is it the forest's fault that something evil had made it it's home? Is it the woodland that is the horror or the unknown and almost unseen that hides within its greenery?

Without spoiling the book for you, they do beat the rats (again), and it is the final line that I wanted to quote:

A breeze sprang up and it seemed to Pender, who was gazing back through an open window at the vermin's funeral pyre, that the very trees were breathing a gentle sigh of relief. (pg 242).

What is always good about a book like this and makes it even more hard hitting is when genuine locations are used. In a note at the end of the book Herbert addresses this, the conservation centre, The Warren, the police training centre at Lippitts Hill, and the church at High Beech - many of which I mention in this book myself – are all real. The house where he bases the vermin's lair is fictitious, but...it is based on a real property which in 1979 when the book was released was a burned-out ruin. I will not say exactly the building which it is because now, you will find quite a grand conversion of apartments of which I would not even want to guess the cost to live in, but if you read or have already read the rest of this book, you may be able to add two and two and work out which it could be.

I did tell you at the beginning that the books I was going to mention are all very different, and the next one is historical fiction written by Adam Foulds, *'The Quickening Maze'*. This is more recent than *Lair*, having been published in 2010 but also uses real places and even more, genuine people who actually existed.

In Foulds' novel we are introduced to a much more personal Dr. Matthew Allen (yes, he of Fairmead House and its neighbour buildings), although the author does allude to the Doctor's failings and lack of monetary acumen that caused his widow to have to sell everything they owned after he died, but enough of that particular plot spoiler.

The main focus in this book is that of poet John Clare. He is described in other works as a *"small sensitive man with keen eyes, high forehead and fine features"* (Epping Forest, William Addison, page 159). Clare could be seen as someone who perhaps had a very tentative grip on reality, with a mental health problem being just around the corner at any one point in time, his sudden rise to fame, and then just as fast fall from the limelight that sent him in a downward spiral, which ended up with him staying at Dr. Allen's facility in the beautiful Epping Forest.

Clare carried on writing (which *The Quickening Maze* mentions), much of his work did not appear to give hint to the mental turmoil he was suffering:

I love the forest and its airy bounds,
Where friendly Campbell takes his daily rounds
I love the breakneck hills, that headlong go
And leave me high and half the world below.

It gives you a good feeling, makes you sense pleasure and happiness, but the Clare in the book does not seem as appreciative of the treatment he is receiving at the asylum. After one sojourn into the woods where he has been bare knuckle boxing with the gypsies who made the forest one of their temporary homes, he is stopped by Dr. Allen and placed into a secure room, responding with "You cannot cage a man, you cannot, I'll tear this door down."

It is interesting that in his real-life writings and in this fictional account of his time in Epping Forest, he was always looking for escape. Did he see a chance to embrace his wanderlust by almost living vicariously through the travelling Romany folk? Or were they his key to freedom? He definitely had a strong connection to the forest, as shown in a poem he wrote when a thunder storm had broken over the area:

Roll on, ye wrath of thunders, peal on peal

Till worlds are ruins, and myself alone
Melt heart and soul, cased in obdurate steel
Till I can feel that nature is my throne.

The theme of freedom runs through him, one of his goals during the novel (and in fact, in real life) was to escape back home to Northampton - he had visions of his wife Patty, speaking with her about their children, and trying to explain to her how his former home meant freedom. As with anyone trying to be logical with someone who can only comprehend the illogical, he envisages her saying "Why do you want to come home? The people aren't free there either."
"But they're not shut up, they're not locked away." Maybe this is the author trying to understand how someone with reduced capacity for competent thought would argue with himself and could also be a view on how nature is being treated as he says "The land is fenced, can't walk across nothing, we're kept in narrow tracks. The common land is owned. The poor are driven away, the gypsies also." (*The Quickening Maze*, page 181).

Whilst those of you who know about John Clare, and just why he was hospitalised in the first place will be aware of the fact that he believed himself to be many other people – Lord Byron and Shakespeare are just two of the most famous names whose work he took credit for, whether he believed he was them or had been them in a past life is uncertain, although as Byron died in 1824, and was born only five years before Clare, it is virtually impossible that he was the "reincarnation" as some have written.

He did "escape" the asylum however which is written in a beautiful way and infers almost that the forest was a prison (something we shall look at in the next book as well), but the author is hinting at that the woods were not quite ready to let him go:

"He left the forest, the doctor, the other patients, Stockdale's tortures behind him. He broke through the incessant rushing sound of the trees into silence" and then "he had to choose a road for Enfield, and took the wrong one..." (page 253). Normally an area so chock-full of nature would be the peaceful place, the quiet zone, the area of tranquillity, but in this person's mind, the forest is the noisy and disruptive place.

The next novel I chose which features the woods in all their splendour (and with a fantastical imagination to boot) is 'The Clocks in this House All Tell Different Times' by Xan Brooks. I can say, hand on heart, that this book did not go in the direction I imagined it to. Having read the reviews before picking up a copy, one really called out to me by Alex Preston, the author of 'In Love and War'. He said "A fairy tale wrapped within a historical novel." Fantastic, I thought, just the kind of thing I enjoy reading as I knew it was set initially in the summer of 1923 and featured injured soldiers of the Great War - and I do mean injured in myriad ways and not just the obvious.

The work starts with a section entitled 'The Forest' and straight to Epping we go. The main character, a teenage orphan called Lucy is telling us, the reader, that it is an honour to be invited to the woods, the way her grandmother is fussing over her hair, allowing her to wear her precious "nice" dress, and even acting like it is a non-descript, childlike play date when she returns home and exchanges pleasantries with her nan. Even when you find out that her weekly Sunday sojourn on a rickety old army lorry is to meet with four injured, former World War One fighters with the group moniker of the "Funny Men", and individual nicknames of Toto, Tin Man, Scarecrow and Lion – yes, the Wizard of Oz reference just adds to the mystical illusion – you still do not think anything unseemly is going on.

These regular meetings always take place in the privacy of Epping Forest, a place that the author likens to "a journey back to the distant past." (page 8). Is he comparing the woods and nature to a type of time machine where the injured "funny men" can forget about their wounds and be happy? This certainly seems to be the magic of the forest, shown by another line "the world regresses, grows younger...". Moving away from the book for a short while, how many of us suddenly feel like children again when in the woods, stomping through the mud, or kicking the fallen leaves? Or picking up a stick and swooshing it through the air as though it is a mighty broad sword? I do not believe you if you say that is just me!

There is so much description in the early chapters to make you believe that the bevy of trees and nature has magical powers: "...enter the fantastical forest where anything can happen" and "It exists outside time", but when you compare it to Lucy's actual home, where she is an orphan with her brother, her grandparents pub that is slowly dying and the street is failing, it is a stark contrast to the renewal of health and vigour that we see in the forest.

This magical view of the forest being a return to childhood (not even a return for Lucy, she is only around fourteen years old), we find it is so much darker than that and rather than it being for rejuvenation, it is nothing more than a game of hide and seek – which you soon come to realise is a euphemism for sex, and that these four children, of which three are teenage girls, and one a young boy, are being pimped out by their guardians for money, of which they see none.

Without ruining the book for you – I did enjoy it, well perhaps enjoy is the wrong word as I felt very uncomfortable at children being treated as sex toys - two of girls even become christened "pleasure dolls" towards the end, although not by any of the Wizard of Oz characters. There is another character, Arthur Elms, a different Great War veteran who is obese, described as repulsive and able to conjure flames from his fingers. His memories of the war seem to produce elation in him as opposed to sadness or trauma, however I do wonder if the author is trying to intimate that all was not well in Elms' mind beforehand, and that all the horror he experienced, was misfiled almost in his brain.

Once they leave the safety and seclusion of the magical forest, things begin to go wrong for our troop, people run away, people die (although the "Funny Men" were already classed as dead which is why they were not with their families, one preferring his wife to have his death benefits rather than having to cope on a miniscule war pension and be faced with his disfigured visage every day), but some are reborn. This may seem strange, but not once did I "blame" the four veterans for having sex with these children, that is not how the author has written it - the criticism and reproach is laid squarely on those accepting the money. It may be the romantic way it is written, which I am sure is intentional, rather than a sentence which says "the man in the tin mask forced the young fourteen-year-old girl behind the tree, pushed her down, and raped her...".

If that is not enough to make you want to read it, there is also a jazz band from Tennessee, a very big house (which is crumbling down), a lunatic posh boy and quite a lot of murder...

So far, we have seen the forest used as a quasi-prison (in John Clare's eyes), a battlefield for vermin (*Lair*) and a fantasy land where anything goes (*The Clocks in this House...*), what is next?

Those who know me are probably aware that I am not a huge fan of Charles Dickens. Apart from his disgusting treatment of his wife Catherine, also his total arrogance, I will begrudgingly admit that he wrote the odd good book or two... (yes, that is said tongue in cheek).

Whilst he said of one then-town in Essex "If any one were to ask me what in my opinion was the dullest and most stupid spot on the face of the Earth, I should decidedly say Chelmsford", he was a fan of another part of the county, that of Chigwell and Epping Forest, and he wrote his novel '*Barnaby Rudge'* in that very area.

I find with books by Dickens, you must plough through the first third or so before the storyline really starts to grip you (a very wise friend, thank you Lorna, also agreed with me on that point, and if she says so, it is true) and *Barnaby Rudge* is no different. The saga is set in the late 1700's and is establishing a baseline to talk about the anti-popery riots of 1780, something which I admit I was not familiar with until reading this - do not make me compliment Dickens on developing my knowledge of history...please.

This tale opens with a description of an inn called The Maypole, but what is interesting is that whilst there definitely was a hostelry of this name in Chigwell, it is not that one which Dickens is describing. The pub is more commonly known as The Kings Head, or for those who watch "TOWIE", the restaurant-bar better known as Sheesh.

Postcard authors own, stamped January 1907

So you can visit Chigwell and step into both historical and quite current media type fame.

The proprietor of the Old Maypole is a contradictory fellow by the name of John Willett, he treats his son Joe like a juvenile idiot, and positively brown noses the landowners nearby. I will not go through every single character, but there are those that you wish to come to a sticky end (Chester) and even those who you know are devious and deserving of punishment, but you wonder exactly why they are built that way (Hugh, believe it or not). The Forest of Essex is painted as both a dark, potentially scary and quite possibly dangerous place, especially for lone riders and walkers, with the ever-present threat of highway robbery. On the flipside, it also seems to be a barrier between the secrets and lives of those in Chigwell, to the dirt and more obvious corruption of nearby London.

There are so many different elements thrown into this book that it is impossible to cover all of them, but there is love, murder and even the debunking of a ghost sighting...yes, Dickens was showing how not everything was paranormal in the 19th century. The character Solomon Daisy, the parish clerk, comes rushing into the Maypole on the twenty-seventh anniversary of the murder of local landowner Reuben Haredale and his steward Rudge (purportedly done by the gardener), absolutely terrified that he has seen the ghost of one of the two men murdered on the 19th March in his churchyard whilst winding up the old clock.

"It was bareheaded to the storm. It turned its face without stopping, and fixed its eyes on mine. It was a ghost – a spirit." (*Barnaby Rudge*, page 266.)

 John Willett chooses to tell Geoffrey Haredale (the late Reuben's brother) of the sighting, and it is the latter who decides to keep it secret.

The reader knows it is not a ghost, but Rudge Senior, the steward they all thought had been murdered - you can probably guess the plot twist. Describing the streets of London, Dickens says: "...they were, one and all, from the broadest and best to the narrowest and least frequented, very dark." (B. R. page 132), juxtapose that with Haredale and his description of Chigwell and The Maypole when he returns from the drama and horrors of the No Popery Riots "It is some comfort to know that everything will not be blighted hereabouts. I shall be glad to have one picture of life and cheerfulness to turn to in my mind." (B.R. page 636.)

I do not want to spoil it for those of you who may choose to read this novel of Dickens' which is probably the least well known, and also perhaps the most complicated storyline to follow! But all the way through is the mention of Grip, the pet raven of the eponymous main character of the novel. As someone who is quite scared of birds anyway, the thought of a huge raven appearing on every page is enough to turn the book into a horror, but we know that Dickens had pet ravens of his own and there are many who believe that Grip was there to be a slightly devilish overseer on Barnaby, with lines like "never say die, bow wow wow, I'm a devil, I'm a devil, I'm a devil - hurrah!" (B.R. page 61), this may not be too far from the truth. For those wondering, this was written around four years before Poe's infamous tale 'The Raven', and Dickens' pet raven had been called Grip too.

Whatever the hidden meaning behind much of Barnaby Rudge, there is no disputing that Dickens had a love for the Epping Forest area (well, Chigwell) hence choosing it to be the primary location for this book.

I could not make up my mind which work to feature last in this chapter, but I decided that the final paragraphs should be for a lady who is said to have been one of the best crime writers ever (and the awards she won are indicative of that), and was also born just on the outskirts of the forest and grew up in places like Loughton and Chigwell, Ruth Rendell.

Whilst having a Dickens book (that uses fifty words when only two are probably needed) and Ruth Rendell who is more likely to get to the point an awful lot quicker, is in direct contrast, it is no less worthy of mention. The Rendell novel I chose was one of her last works before she passed away in 2015, *'The Girl Next Door'*. We are introduced to a Loughton experiencing the complications of World War Two, children playing in places that 21st century parents would have kittens if they found their offspring larking around in (I did try and find a more technical and scholarly term for that, but I thought, why pretend?) people going missing and not much being done about it, and what seems like a general blind eye being turned towards misdemeanours that in times of peace may be more heavily investigated.

"They were on the edge of Essex, an outer suburb of London on the borders of Epping Forest. Green meadows still remained, divided by tall thick hedges composed of many varieties of trees…" (page 14, *The Girl Next Door*).

Whilst the forest is rarely mentioned throughout the book, it is the constant backdrop to the events that come back to haunt the then children of the "qanats" (the tunnels that they played in, which were actually foundations of a house that had stopped building work due to the war breaking out). Whilst Rendell was very much a crime and suspense writer, and not of the historical fiction persuasion, she does write about things that were very much of the time. She mentions people leaving Loughton when the new post-war Debden estate was being constructed, these were places designed to accommodate the East End population who had seen their homes both decimated and also condemned, but those who tried to go a bit further into Essex, with districts like Epping and Theydon Bois welcoming them were "to be deterred by the coming of Harlow New Town. Nimby was a word that was unknown then, but Nimby's were what they were." (P.33, TGND).

It's ironic that my grandparents were some of those people who moved to Harlow in the 1950s, not because of being bombed out of East end properties, but due to the opportunities which were on offer to new residents and the kind of house that was full of the mod cons. Although technically speaking, Harlow existed long before the new town development (now more of an old town, life moves on...) it was not the sprawling conurbation you see now.

An observation I made whilst reading the book – whether intentional on the author's part or not, I do not know – was that it seemed that those former residents who left Loughton had a more exciting life than those who stayed. I think of Alan and Rosemary (if you read it, you will know what I mean). He married the woman who was nearby but maybe not the one who excited him (although he does realise that stability is sexy, only too late). Michael is sent away as a young child to live with his father's cousin and has a much better life than he would have had if he had stayed in Loughton with his parent, Mrs. Moss had never remarried after losing her husband in the early years of the war and remained in her home. Saying that however, Daphne - who to many may seem the most exciting of all the characters — is quite damaged herself, and even leaving the scene has not mended her, so maybe there is just as much validity in staying put to moving on.

The area of the Forest of Essex and its associated living spaces provide both a cover for crime, and also emotions in this book, and it shows it was written by someone who knew the territory well.

Bibliography

The Forest of Essex – William Richard Fisher

Epping Forest – William Addison

Maynard Concise History of Epping Forest – J Maynard

Magna Carta 1215 AD

The Forest Charter 1217 AD

Discovering Highwaymen - Russell Ash

Gentleman Rogues & Wicked Ladies – Fiona McDonald

Essay on the Classification of the Insane – Matthew Allen, MD

Lair – James Herbert

The Quickening Maze – Adam Foulds

Barnaby Rudge – Charles Dickens

The Clocks in this House All Tell Different Times – Xan Brooks

Keepers, Cockneys and Kitchen Maids – Georgina Green

Not all Airmen fly – Jenny Filby & Geoff Clark

The Girl Next Door – Ruth Rendell

Essex Days of Old – Edited by John Page

The Chronicle of Robert of Gloucester

The Elements of Epping Forest

Luftwaffe ranks

Oberleutnant – Oblt – Flying Officer

Leutnant – Lt – Pilot Officer

Feldwebel – FW – Flight Sergeant

Gefreiter – Gefr – Leading Airman

Unteroffizier – Uffr – Corporal

Thanks & Stuff

As someone who openly admits to having flunked her History A Level in spectacular style, it might seem odd that I have chosen a path that means I have to immerse myself in that very subject! For anyone who wants to know, I have always loved learning about the past and finding ways of explaining it, and that is why I have chosen to write my books and talk history to anyone who will listen.

This book would not have seen the light of day if it was not for my friend Jayne Harris (off the telly…it is how she is greeted, I believe it is in her contract) firstly giving me the opportunity to be on Help! My House Is Haunted and the amount of interesting information I discovered whilst researching for that. I am so grateful to her for encouraging me and writing the foreword to this particular piece of work!

Next, all the people who helped with research and investigating this book, the amazing NPAS team at Lippitt's Hill, you guys do an amazing job, Pete, Mark, Mel and Keith of Paracom – thank you so much for your time on this, Essex Records Office for not treating me like a blonde idiot when I could not find the record I was looking for (and also not judging me when I was geeking out over some of the original designs I saw), The National Archives – amazing place, the staff there are so helpful and patient.

Editor Lucy, I am learning I promise! To Andy, my amazing cover designer, I truly love your work.

Lastly, to my family, my husband, two sons and even the dog, you guys have the patience to accompany me on my little adventures and even join in when needed, I know that Loki (the dog) appreciated visiting the forest maybe more than certain other members of our little team but I truly appreciate and love you all.

If I have forgotten anyone I am truly sorry, blame my middle aged brain!

The Elements of Epping Forest

Printed in Great Britain
by Amazon

48084590R00119